GRILL EVERY DAY

125 FAST-TRACK RECIPES FOR WEEKNIGHTS AT THE GRILL

by Diane Morgan

PHOTOGRAPHS BY
E.J. ARMSTRONG

CHRONICLE BOOKS

SAN FRANCISCO

To Greg, Eric, and Molly,
you enrich my life and
make me happy every day.

Library of Congress Cataloging-in-Publication Data available.

ISBN 978-0-8118-5208-1

Manufactured in Hong Kong.

Food styling by Patty Wittmann
Designed by Alicia Nammacher
Typesetting by Connie Bigelow

The photographer wishes to thank
Super Duper Kitchen Styling Backup: Charlotte Omnes
Super Assistant / Digital Saviour: Lance Hofstad

10 9 8 7 6 5 4 3 2 1

Chronicle Books LLC
680 Second Street
San Francisco, California 94107

www.chroniclebooks.com

ACKNOWLEDGMENTS

A true pleasure at the end of writing a book is taking time to thank all the people who have guided me, advised me, supported me, and kept me on track.

To Bill LeBlond, my editor at Chronicle Books and dear friend, for all his expert guidance, support, and time. It's a professional relationship beyond compare and one I cherish deeply.

To Lisa Ekus, my agent, for her amazing advice and enthusiasm. And to Jane Falla and everyone else at The Lisa Ekus Group for their dedicated support.

To Amy Treadwell, Leslie Jonath, Andrea Burnett, Peter Perez, and the others at Chronicle Books, who have inspired, supported, publicized, and otherwise kept my projects on track. You are all delightful to work with. To Sharon Silva, many thanks for copyediting my book with such care and precision. Alicia Nammacher, your book design enhances the words on the page—thank you.

To Cheryl Russell, my fabulous assistant, I don't know what I'd do without you! We've grilled together through rain and shine. You make developing and testing recipes both a pleasure and loads of fun.

To my friends Harriet and Peter Watson, who have eaten more test recipes and given me honest feedback for more books than I can recall. I can't hug and thank you enough. Your friendship and unswerving support bring me joy and much laughter even when deadlines are looming.

Many thanks to my friends, family, and colleagues: David Watson, Paola Gentry and Eric Watson, Richard and Barb LevKoy, Domenica Marchetti, Charlie and Jeanne Sosland, Bruce and Ellen Birenboim, Steve and Marci Taylor, Sukey and Gil Garcetti, Roxane and Austin Huang, Karen Fong, Sherry Gable, Margie Sanders, Ken Sanders, Priscilla and John Longfield, Brijesh and Ann Anand, Deb and Ron Adams, Summer Jameson, Kam and Tony Kimball, Mary and Jack Barber, Sara and Erik Whiteford, Tori Ritchie, Josie Jimenez, Joyce Goldstein, John Ash, Monica Bhide, Denise Bina, Judith Bishop, Carolyn Burleigh, Ericka Carlson, Lisa Hill, Jamie Purviance, Rick Rodgers, Lisa Donoughe, Kathy Campbell, Barbara Dawson and Matthew Katzer, Tony Gemignani, Braiden Rex-Johnson, Alma Lach, Michael Wehman, Janine MacLachlan, Laura Werlin, Andy Schloss, and Cathy Whims.

Special thanks to Antonia Allegra and Don and Joan Fry for their professional guidance and encouragement. Whether in France or at the Greenbrier, it is always treasured time when we are together.

Finally, this book wouldn't have been nearly as much fun to write without my loving and nurturing husband, Greg, sharing in all I do. To Eric and Molly, my children, thank you for all your love and caring every step of the way.

CONTENTS

INTRODUCTION

I DIDN'T CONCEIVE OF THIS BOOK WHEN I WAS FOURTEEN YEARS OLD, BUT THAT'S WHEN I BUILT MY FIRST LIVE FIRE. I was spending a month at Camp Barney Medintz in northern Georgia, making friends, building skills, singing spirited songs, and generally enjoying days of structured activities away from my family. I had been an eager camper from the age of six, starting with day camps and then maturing to overnight ones. But I was particularly excited about this summer camp because it included "survival" training, or as much as any camp was going to risk with a bunch of teenagers. Still, we were taught all the skills we needed to exist for one long night in the woods alone. The most important was building a fire—specifically, mastering the one-match fire. I excelled.

Digging a little pit with a shovel and gathering tiny dry twigs, then bigger ones, and finally dead, fallen branches large enough to sustain an ongoing fire for cooking and keeping warm—this was the goal. We were given plenty of instruction and then an in-camp test, our final hurdle before setting off into the woods with minimal provisions, sleeping bag, and tarp. For the test, each camper received three matches, and I immediately started arranging little twigs in a crosshatch pattern, building layers and allowing for critical airflow. Crouched down on my knees, my elbow and forearm resting on the dirt, my cheek next to the ground, I lit a match, placed it under the twigs without hitting the dirt, and waited a minute for the sticks to catch fire. As soon as I saw red-glowing wood, I blew ever so gently to spread the flame without extinguishing it. I did it with one match, and then I was ready to survive on my own, at least the eating part.

After we'd hiked about four miles as a group, the counselors gave us our final instructions and handed out our meager food supplies—a hot dog, a raw baking potato, a package each of instant hot chocolate and oatmeal—and three matches. We all carried a small shovel, ball of twine, Swiss Army knife, whistle, water, metal cup, and spoon. We were separated and told we were to "survive" from afternoon until morning. If something went desperately wrong, we could blow our whistle to signal for help.

I felt rugged, ready, and capable. I was in touch with that primordial link to my prehistoric roots. I gathered wood, built a lean-to for my night's shelter, and began to dig the fire pit. Fortunately, I didn't have to hunt for my dinner! A one-match fire fueled my ego, so to speak, but it also meant I could grill a hot dog on a stick and wrap my potato in leaves, letting it bake under the coals. I watched the stars and sang to myself well into the dark, smoke-scented night. Sleep was fitful, as I was sure I was going to be eaten by a hungry creature. I couldn't wait for daylight, and the chance to start another fire.

This was the beginning of my love of building fires, but it took time to translate this youthful passion for flames into grilling. When I was growing up, my father manned the backyard grill, and I was assigned the boring job of setting the table and folding the napkins. When my culinary career began, I was an apartment dweller without a place to put even a hibachi. This was Chicago, and we all know what happened when Mrs. O'Leary's cow kicked over the lantern. Fire laws were strict, so you couldn't put a grill on any fire escape. It wasn't until I moved to Portland, Oregon, that I began my outdoor culinary adventures. My husband bought me a grill as a birthday present *and* he assembled it. I realize this is not every girl's idea of a romantic gift, but it pleased me.

I became the weekend grill warrior, the tamer of the flame, the twenty-pound-charcoal-bag-haulin' ma'am, the backyard-grill party gal, and the smokin' Thanksgiving-turkey-on-the-grill queen. And, finally, I turned that obsession into my sixth cookbook and first grill book, *Dressed to Grill*, published in 2002. Since then, I've incorporated as many grill recipes into my other cookbooks as I could: turkey on the grill, salmon on the grill, pizza on the grill.

Now comes *Grill Every Day: 125 Fast-Track Recipes for Weeknights at the Grill*. The progression makes sense to me now. The idea for this book came on a flight home after teaching cooking classes in Texas. I was looking at my calendar and thinking ahead to all I had to do and manage the coming week. I had work to catch up on, plus I had my children's sports games to attend, which always cramp the dinner hour. I needed quick meals with virtually no cleanup. I would grill. In fact, I would grill almost every night—quick, easy foods that didn't take a lot of prep or cooking. Pretty soon I was building a repertoire of interesting grilled meat, fish, poultry, vegetable, and even dessert recipes that were doable on a week-night. My friends wanted recipes; my editor wanted recipes and a book proposal!

Grill Every Day is all about grilling. (I save barbecuing—with its long marinating times, low fires, smoking techniques, and hunks of meat tended for hours—for weekends.) It is the ultimate practical guide for anyone who wants to put a fabulous-tasting meal on the table and have virtually no pots and pans to wash. With grilling, there's not even a stove to scrub—just a grill grate to brush clean!

You'll find tips on how to make quick work of cleaning that grate, plus all the other basics, in Chapter 1 (page 12). For folks with a gas grill, I have included the ins and outs of lighting, controlling, and maintaining it. There's also an extensive section on charcoal grills, with information on building a fire and choosing the best fuel. And for anyone who wants to buy a first grill or a new grill, I discuss the pros and cons of gas and charcoal grills. The must-have tools section gives you a critical list of what to buy in addition to what might be just plain fun to own. (I've noticed grillers tend to be gadget buyers, too.)

A well-stocked grill pantry is the key to successful—and easygoing—grilling. For me, this includes homemade sauces and rubs, plus a great combination of store-bought sauces, spices, and rubs. My grilling season begins when I make a triple batch of my Grill Every Day Spice Rub (page 31) for the pantry. Simple pork tenderloin turns into a lip-buzzing meal when it's coated with Latin Spice Rub (page 32), while alder-planked salmon dazzles when it's doused with a lemon-vodka-dill marinade (page 84) that's as simple to make as a martini (another good idea after a long day of work!). Or, consider kicking up the flavor of chicken breasts by drizzling them with Moroccan Pesto (page 115) when they come off the grill. Chapter 2, The Grill Pantry (page 28) is filled with big-flavored sauces and rubs that help guarantee easy-to-make weeknight meals.

The recipes in this book, which have all been family- and friend-tested, celebrate rich flavors and global tastes. You'll see classics with a twist, such as a rib-eye steak with some cowboy ingenuity (page 46), or a big burger stuffed with blue cheese (page 52). For lamb lovers, check out the Asian-inspired Lemongrass-Grilled Lamb Loin Chops (page 61), or ask your butcher to cut lamb steaks from the leg and grill Mediterranean-influenced Mustard-and-Rosemary-Crusted Lamb Steaks (page 57). For the calorie-conscious with global taste buds, grilling is the ticket to lean meals with heady, vibrant flavors. Turn to page 89 and discover Salmon Grilled on a Bed of Herbs, or try Orange-and-Chipotle-Rubbed Chicken Breasts (page 117).

I'm a huge fan of vegetables on the grill and have included fifteen recipes, plus a number of vegetarian main courses (especially to please my daughter). This grill book wouldn't be complete without two other additions: a collection of accompaniments that I call Treasured Sides (page 166), and a chapter titled The Grill Planner—Second Helpings (page 182) that utilizes leftovers. Firing up the grill once and grilling enough food for one night's meal, plus extras for creative leftovers, makes for smarter weeknight cooking. For a sweet finale, I have included a big chapter called Fire-Roasted Fruits and Other Sweet Treats (page 202). After all, who can resist grilled peaches and pears, or Dark Chocolate S'Mores Sundaes (page 212)? Not me!

I wish someone had given me a big, gooey sundae with grilled marshmallows that night when I was fourteen, building a one-match fire and surviving in the woods alone. But for me, so many years later, the thrill of the grill burns on. Whether I am flicking a switch to light my gas grill or piling a bunch of charcoal in a chimney starter and using one match to light my charcoal grill, I get to be outside, see flames flickering, and know that I can make a wonderful meal in no time at all. To me, that translates to great fun and great food every night of the week.

Happy Grilling!

GRILLING BASICS FOR THE WEEKNIGHT COOK

ALL ABOUT GRILLS

Purchasing a grill, like buying any appliance, involves thoughtful decision-making. The big decision, of course, is whether to buy a gas grill, a charcoal grill, or what I call a hybrid: a charcoal grill with an attached propane starter. There is no right or wrong answer. Instead, you have to decide what level of convenience you want, because that's what it comes down to. If you think you will grill more often if all you have to do is flick a switch, then buy a gas grill. On the other hand, if you like building a fire, tinkering with the flames, and experimenting with different types of fuel, then go with a charcoal grill.

Purists insist that charcoal grills rule, but I believe that whatever gets you grilling most often is what makes the decision. I own several grills, and find myself using one or another depending on the day's circumstances and what I am trying to grill. If I need the grill for only fifteen minutes for some chicken breasts, then I'm likely to use the gas grill. However, if I plan to grill a main dish, some vegetables, and then some grill-roasted apples for dessert, I light the charcoal grill. Know thyself! What follows is a detailed explanation of gas and charcoal grills to help you make your decision.

GAS GRILLS

BUYING A GAS GRILL: QUALITY, FEATURES, AND SIZE

Owning a gas grill is all about convenience. With either a natural-gas hookup or a refillable propane tank, a gas grill is heated and ready for grilling within 15 to 20 minutes of flicking the switch. Gas grills typically have either inverted V-shaped metal bars, ceramic briquettes, or crushed lava stones, with gas jets underneath that create intense heat. As the sizzling juices and fat drip down, smoke is created, flavoring the foods. Excess grease is channeled down to a catch pan with, hopefully, a disposable liner.

Look for a sturdy, well-built grill with a heavy firebox; electronic ignition; separate heating zones (two are okay; three are good; four are even better; six mean you entertain, feed lots of people, and are a serious griller!); burner controls for high, medium, and low; and a built-in thermometer that registers degrees, rather than just high, medium, and low. For a propane grill, a gauge that shows when the tank is low on fuel is helpful, but always having a full backup tank on hand saves the day. (Running out of gas in the middle of grilling is the last thing you want to happen. I know from experience!) If a grill is to last, the burners should be made of stainless steel, and if the grill has V-shaped metal bars, they should be porcelain-enameled steel or stainless steel. Look for grills with quality safety features, such as a device to limit the flow of gas in the event of a hose rupture, a mechanism to shut off the grill, and a feature to prevent the flow of gas if the connection between the tank and the grill is not leakproof.

Most grill grates are made of stainless steel, porcelain-coated cast iron, or just plain steel. A cast-iron grill grate is ideal for all the same reasons a good cast-iron skillet or grill pan is perfect for searing: its surface gets hot and holds its heat, it etches beautiful grill marks onto food, and the food cooks faster the moment it hits the grate. That being said, a cast-iron grate needs to be properly cared for, which means keeping it well oiled and clean so it doesn't rust. Just like a good cast-iron skillet, a cast-iron grill grate, once it is well seasoned, performs beautifully.

New grills come with lots of extras, such as side burners for heating sauces or cooking corn, rotisseries for spit roasting, and built-in metal smoker boxes for wood chips. Having counter space on either side of the grill is incredibly helpful, and some of the newer grills have swing-up counters to give you even more surface area. A grill cover, which offers protection from the weather, is an important accessory because it extends the life of the grill.

Gas grills range in price from a few hundred dollars up to five thousand dollars and more. Most are freestanding units, but with the rise in outdoor kitchens as an entertaining space, many are designed as built-ins. Do some research and buy the best grill you can afford. Look for companies that offer good customer support and warranty packages (see Sources, page 220).

LIGHTING A GAS GRILL

With the flick of a switch, a gas grill is lit, but there are a few safety rules to keep in mind and features to consider. First, make sure the grill lid is open before turning on the gas. If the lid is closed, gas buildup can result in an explosion. If using a propane tank, open the valve at the top of the tank. Look carefully at the manufacturer's instructions, as most gas grills have a designated burner tube that should be lit first. In some instances, depending on the configuration of the grill, a crossover bar sends the flame over to the second burner tube. Set the burner knob to high, press the ignition switch until the burner lights, turn on additional burners if needed, close the lid, and let the grill preheat for 15 to 20 minutes. Once hot, adjust the temperature knobs to the desired level for grilling, and use a grill brush to scrape the grill grate clean. Oil the grate and you are ready to grill.

When you are finished grilling, shut off the gas at the source (at the tank for a propane grill) and then turn the burners to Off (this order ensures the fuel hoses do not remain under pressure). While the grill is still hot, use the wire brush again to clean the grate. Keep the lid open while the grill cools down.

DIRECT GRILLING ON A GAS GRILL

This method is used for foods that cook relatively quickly, such as burgers, steaks, vegetables, fish fillets, and kebabs. As the name implies, you are grilling directly over the lit burners. Set as many burners as you need to the desired temperature. When the grill is fully preheated, place the foods on the grill grate directly over the heated zone.

INDIRECT GRILLING ON A GAS GRILL

This technique is used either for foods that need long, slow cooking—such as a whole chicken, a rack of ribs, or a whole fish—or for foods that are first seared over direct heat and then moved to a cooler zone to finish cooking. It's easy to set up hot and cool zones or even three temperature zones on a gas grill, though your grill must have at least two burners to make it possible. For a two-burner grill, light one burner and keep the other burner turned off. For a three-burner grill, either light the left and right burner and leave the center burner off, or light the front and back burners and leave the center burner off. For a four-burner grill, light the outside burners and leave the two center burners off, or light the two left burners and leave the two right burners off. Since all the recipes in this book are for quick weeknight meals, I use this indirect technique only for foods that are seared over direct heat and then finished over a cool zone, such as chicken thighs or a butterflied chicken.

Most gas grills, depending on the number of burners, light from either left to right or front to back. I own a four-burner gas grill that lights from left to right, which I think offers the best flexibility for creating hot and cool zones for indirect grilling. I find the easiest method is to light the two outer burners and have the two center burners off. Grills that light from front to back offer less flexibility, because the center section is too narrow to grill particularly large items, such as a turkey.

TEMPERATURE CONTROL ON A GAS GRILL

Just as your gas grill allows you to establish different temperature zones for indirect grilling, it also lets you create hot, medium, and cool zones for greater flexibility and control for direct grilling. This means that if foods are searing too quickly and the center has not cooked through, you can move them from a hot zone to a medium or cool zone. To achieve this variety of heat levels, preheat the grill until hot, then set the burners to different temperatures.

Even though gas grills boast of even heat distribution, I have never cooked on one that didn't have one or more hot and/or cool spots. As with a new oven, it takes time to learn a grill's quirks and to figure out the adjustments necessary to achieve even grilling. Below is a chart with general temperature guidelines for gas grills. To use the hand test, hold your hand about 4 inches above the grill grate and count off seconds: "one thousand one, one thousand two, one thousand three," and so on, to determine how hot the grill is.

HEAT	TEMPERATURE	BURNER SETTING	HAND TEST
HIGH	450° TO 650°F	HIGH	1 TO 2 SECONDS
MEDIUM-HIGH	400° TO 425°F	MEDIUM-HIGH	3 TO 4 SECONDS
MEDIUM	350° TO 375°F	MEDIUM	4 TO 5 SECONDS
MEDIUM-LOW	300° TO 325°F	MEDIUM-LOW	5 TO 6 SECONDS
LOW	225° TO 275°F	LOW	7 SECONDS OR MORE

A clean grill is a well-functioning, well-performing grill. Follow the manufacturer's instructions for cleaning the grill annually or semiannually (depending on how much you grill). This involves turning off the gas supply; taking off the grill grate and brushing it; removing the V-shaped metal bars, ceramic briquettes, or lava stones covering the burners and brushing them clean; lightly brushing the burner tubes to make sure all the gas ports are clean and open; cleaning the bottom of the grill and the grease-collection tray; and replacing the disposable pan (if needed). If you have what looks like peeling black paint on the grill lid or grill bottom, use a bristle brush or putty knife to scrape off the flakes. This is buildup of carbon from the accumulated cooking vapors. Put everything back together and you are ready to grill.

Every time you use the grill, first check the grease-collection tray to make sure it is not full. (A grease fire under a lit gas grill is dangerous.) Once the grill is preheated, brush the grate with a grill brush. The burnt bits of food from the last time you grilled loosen more easily when the grate is hot. Oil the grate before grilling. If you have time, brush the grate again once you have turned off the grill.

 ## CHARCOAL GRILLS

BUYING A CHARCOAL GRILL: QUALITY, FEATURES, AND SIZE

Nothing beats the basic kettle-style grill for cost and quality. It's well priced, sturdy, and easy to use, and often comes with a good warranty and a helpful customer-support line. It can be used for direct grilling and indirect grilling, and because of the height of the domed lid, it can accommodate even a large turkey for grill-roasting. The best models have a hinged grate for easy access to the coals, a grate at the bottom for holding the charcoal, an ash catcher, vents at the bottom for airflow, a lid with vents, and, ideally, a temperature gauge and side baskets to hold coals for indirect grilling.

When it comes to grilling, size does matter. If you live in an apartment and have space only for a hibachi or tabletop grill on your balcony or patio, then a small grill will get the job done, allowing you to savor the flavors from live charcoal grilling. However, if you have room, a larger model will give you more versatility and will include key features that add considerable pleasure to the grilling experience. A kettle-style grill built into a large, attached table makes grilling easier, because you have a place to set tools and food containers right next to the grill. Balancing tools and pans on a chair or deck railing, as I have done many times, is a juggling act that can result in spilled and dropped items.

Chimney and electric starters are easy enough to use, but I have been most impressed with what I call the hybrid grill. Made by Weber, this charcoal grill with a propane starter gives me the best of both worlds: I can grill over a live charcoal fire and enjoy the ease of starting the fuel with propane. The hybrid is more expensive than a simple kettle grill, but its advantages go beyond easy igniting. The propane starter is set under the tabletop, which means there's counter space next to the grill, plus there's a large hinged container on the side for storing charcoal (see Sources, page 220).

Charcoal grills that allow you to move either the cooking grate or the charcoal grate up and down give you better temperature control than kettle-style grills. But because kettle-style grills have plenty of space between the charcoal and the cooking grate, you can build a two- or three-zone fire, which permits another form of control. Do some research and buy the best charcoal grill you can afford. Look for companies that offer good customer support and warranty packages.

Let's talk about fuel first. As far as charcoal goes, three choices are available. First, there is lump hardwood charcoal, also known as charwood or chunk charwood charcoal. This fuel is pure charcoal: irregularly shaped lumps of fragrant hardwood, free of impurities. Mesquite is the most common charwood on the market, but alder, hickory, apple, cherry, pecan, and oak are also available. Charwood burns hotter and faster at the start and then loses heat; watch it closely for sparks. It imparts a woodsy flavor to foods.

Second, there are pillow-shaped, chemical-free natural briquettes made from pulverized charwood. They make a good fire, though they are more expensive than composition briquettes, the third fuel choice. These latter briquettes, commonly known as charcoal briquettes, are readily available and produce a good, steady fire that doesn't pop or spark. They are made from charred hardwood, coal, and lignite, molded together with starch binders. I prefer briquettes that do not have lighter fluid added. Kingsford Charcoal with Sure Fire Grooves is a relatively new briquette on the market. These grooved pillows have more edges and surface area, which allows them to catch the flame more quickly, making them easier and faster to light. The additional air channels also mean the briquettes burn hotter and are ready for grilling sooner. They have become my briquette of choice for weeknight grilling, because the coals are ready within 20 minutes of when I light the charcoal. If I want to instill a woodsy flavor in whatever I am grilling, I mix a few pieces of charwood into the briquettes.

The quantity of charcoal you need depends on the size of your grill and how much food you will be grilling. Start with enough to cover the charcoal grate in a single layer. You can always replenish with more charcoal as needed. Here are a few guidelines: A 6-quart chimney starter filled to the top holds 5½ to 6 pounds of charcoal or about 90 briquettes and will cover a 22½-inch kettle-style grill with almost a double layer of coals. This provides about 1¼ hours of cooking time. A chimney starter filled two-thirds full holds roughly 4 pounds of charcoal, or 60 briquettes. This is enough charcoal to cover the charcoal grate of a

CLOCKWISE, FROM ABOVE:

MESQUITE-LUMP
HARDWOOD CHARCOAL

NATURAL WOOD CHIPS, FOR
IMPARTING WOOD-SMOKE
FLAVOR TO GRILLED FOODS

CHIMNEY STARTER WITH
PILLOW-SHAPED CHEMICAL-FREE
NATURAL BRIQUETTES

$22^{1}/_{2}$-inch kettle-style grill with a single layer of coals and provides about 45 minutes of cooking time. A $14^{1}/_{4}$-inch kettle-style grill needs about 2 pounds of charcoal, or 30 briquettes, to cover the grate with a single layer of coals and provides about 45 minutes of cooking time. The weight of the charcoal will vary depending on the type of fuel used.

There are four ways to start a charcoal fire: a chimney starter, an electric starter, a built-in propane starter, or my least favorite way (but it works)—a wad of newspapers. Keep in mind that if you are using Kingsford Charcoal with Sure Fire Grooves for any of these methods, the coals will be ready in just under 20 minutes. To build a fire using a chimney starter, turn the can upside down and fill the lower chamber with crumpled newspapers. Turn the chimney right side up and fill it with charcoal. Place the can on the charcoal grate, open the vents on the bottom of the grill, and light the newspaper through the vent holes near the base of the chimney. The coals are ready to dump in the grill when they glow orange-red and the ones on top are covered with fine gray ash. This takes 20 to 25 minutes. Arrange the coals on the charcoal grate, oil the cooking grate, allow the cooking grate to heat up for 5 to 10 minutes, and you are ready to grill. A word of caution: Do not use self-igniting charcoal (containing lighter fluid) with a chimney starter.

To start a charcoal fire with an electric starter, use a heavy-duty extension cord or move the grill to a safe location near an electrical outlet. Open the vents on the bottom of the grill, arrange the charcoal in a pile on the charcoal grate, and nestle the electric starter between the layers of charcoal. Plug the starter into the electrical outlet. After about 20 minutes, the majority of the coals will be blazing and covered with gray ash. Remove the starter and find a safe, heatproof place away from children and pets to let it cool down. Arrange the coals on the charcoal grate, oil the cooking grate, and allow the cooking grate to heat up for 5 to 10 minutes. Again, do not use self-igniting charcoal with an electric starter.

If you purchased a charcoal grill with a propane starter, follow the manufacturer's instructions for lighting the charcoal. It is usually as simple as opening the vents on the bottom of the grill, arranging the charcoal in a pile on the charcoal grate, turning on the propane starter, and allowing it to ignite the charcoal, which only takes about 5 minutes. The starter is turned off, and the charcoal burns until it turns orange-red and is covered with fine gray ash. This takes 20 to 25 minutes. Arrange the coals on the charcoal grate, oil the cooking grate, and allow the cooking grate to heat up for 5 to 10 minutes. Again, do not use self-igniting charcoal with a propane starter.

The fourth method is basic, but it does work. Open the bottom vents on the grill. Wad a lot of newspaper under the charcoal grate, set the grate in place, and pile charcoal on top. Light the paper. After about 20 minutes, the coals will be orange-red and covered with fine gray ash. Arrange the coals on the charcoal grate, oil the cooking grate, allow the cooking grate to heat up for 5 to 10 minutes, and you are ready to grill. With this method, self-igniting charcoal is safe to use.

This method is used for quick-cooking foods, such as burgers, steaks, vegetables, fish fillets, and kebabs, all of them placed directly over the coals. The coals are spread out below the grill grate, and the air vents at the bottom of the grill and on the lid are wide open. The simplest direct-grilling method is a single-zone fire, which means all the charcoal is in a uniform layer across the charcoal grate. To gain some control, and to create a cool zone in case food begins to burn, rake the coals across the grate but leave a small area coal-free. (See the Temperature Control section below for specifics on creating two- and three-zone fires.)

This technique is typically used for food that either needs long, slow cooking—such as a whole chicken, a rack of ribs, or a whole fish—or is first seared over direct heat and then moved to a cooler zone to finish cooking. It's easy to set up hot and cool zones, or even three temperature zones in a charcoal grill. Partially open the vents at the bottom of the grill, light the coals, and when they are blazing orange-red, mound them against one or both sides of the grill (the choice will depend on the type and design of your grill). Some charcoal grills have special metal baskets at the bottom for holding the coals in the correct position for indirect cooking. Place a drip pan—a disposable rectangular or round aluminum pan—directly below the food to prevent grease flare-ups.

Position the food on the opposite side from the coals or between the mounds of coals. Cover the grill and follow the recipe directions. Since all the recipes in this book are for quick weeknight meals, I use the indirect technique for such foods as chicken thighs or a butterflied chicken that needs to be seared and then finished on the cool side of the grill. Because I am searing them first, I don't need a drip pan when I move the food to the cool zone.

Just as you establish different temperature zones for indirect grilling, you can create hot, medium, and cool zones for greater flexibility and control for direct grilling. This is achieved by banking the coals in different configurations. For a steady, moderate amount of heat, create a single-zone fire by arranging the coals in a single layer across the charcoal grate. To gain some control and to create a cool zone in case food begins to burn, rake the coals across the charcoal grate but leave a small area coal-free. To build a two-zone fire, arrange the coals so there is a double layer of coals on one side of the grill and a single layer on the other side. This allows foods such as chicken thighs, a butterflied chicken, or a pork tenderloin to attain a nice sear on the hot side of the grill and to finish cooking without charring on the cooler area of the grill. For ultimate control, create a three-zone fire, creating a double layer of coals on one side, a single layer in the center, and an area without coals on the other side. I use a three-zone fire when I am cooking a combination of foods, such as chicken and potatoes. I cook the potatoes on the cool side of the grill, while I sear the chicken over the hot zone and then move it to the moderate zone. Once the chicken is seared, I cover the grill and allow the chicken and potatoes to finish cooking.

Below is a chart with general temperature guidelines for charcoal grills. To use the hand test, hold your hand about 4 inches above the grate and count off seconds: "one thousand one, one thousand two, one thousand three, and so on," to determine how hot the grill is.

HEAT	TEMPERATURE	LOOK OF THE COALS	HAND TEST
HIGH	450° TO 650°F	GLOWING ORANGE-RED	1 TO 2 SECONDS
MEDIUM-HIGH	400° TO 425°F	GLOWING ORANGE, SOME ASH	3 TO 4 SECONDS
MEDIUM	350° TO 375°F	GLOWING ORANGE, ASHED OVER	4 TO 5 SECONDS
MEDIUM-LOW	300° TO 325°F	FAINT ORANGE, ASHED OVER	5 TO 6 SECONDS
LOW	225° TO 275°F	FAINT ORANGE, HEAVILY ASHED OVER	7 SECONDS OR MORE

THE SIMPLE RULES OF CHARCOAL GRILL MAINTENANCE

As with a gas grill, a clean charcoal grill is a well-functioning, well-performing grill. Follow the manufacturer's instructions for cleaning the grill annually or semiannually (depending on how much you grill). This involves taking off the grill grate and brushing it, removing the charcoal grate and brushing it, cleaning the bottom of the grill, and cleaning out the ash catcher. If you have what looks like peeling black paint on the lid or the bottom, use a bristle brush or putty knife to scrape off the flakes. This is carbon buildup from the accumulated cooking vapors. Put everything back together and you are ready to grill.

Every time you use the grill, check the ash catcher to make sure it is not full. Once the grill is preheated, brush the cooking grate with a grill brush. The burnt bits of food from the last time you grilled loosen more easily when the grate is hot. Oil the grill grate before grilling. If you have time, brush the grill grate once again when the grill is cool.

 OILING THE GRILL GRATE

There are two effective ways to oil the grill grate on a charcoal or gas grill before you put food on it. The first way is to fill a small bowl with vegetable oil, and fold a paper towel into a small, thick rectangle. Then, grip the towel wad with a pair of long tongs, dip it into the oil just to saturate it, and smear it back and forth along the bars of the grate to grease them. This is a safe and easy method.

The second way is to spray the grate with a high-heat vegetable oil spray. I use a stainless-clad pump spray bottle, purchased at a cookware store, and fill it with grapeseed or canola oil. This way, I'm not dealing with an aerosol can near the fire. Nonetheless, two cautions must be taken: First, you must hold the spray bottle about 10 inches above the grate to keep the can away from the fire. Second, you must spray the grate quickly, starting at the back of the grill. If you start at the front of the grill, you'll have flare-ups at the front as you try to spray the back. Because the oil hitting the charcoal or gas jets will flare momentarily, this technique has a bit of pyrotechnics involved, but it is wonderfully simple. A chemical engineer I know who grills a lot also uses this technique, factoring in the safety tips I have just explained. An alternative, and the absolute safest method, is to use heavy-duty grill mitts and lift the grate off the grill and away from the fire to spray it.

GRILL SAFETY

Whether you are grilling over gas or charcoal, you are playing with a live fire, and safety is of primary importance. Carefully follow these guidelines:

☐ Always have the lid open or off when lighting a grill.

☐ Never leave a fire unattended.

☐ Place your grill on a level, heatproof surface, with no obstructions nearby.

☐ Keep coarse salt handy to smother a fire, as well as a fire extinguisher.

☐ Keep pets and small children away from a lit grill.

☐ Don't wear loose-fitting clothes, and do tie back your hair if it is long.

☐ Find a heatproof spot to cool down the chimney or electric starter after using it.

☐ Check the ash catcher and grease catch pan; empty before lighting the grill.

☐ Let the grill cool completely before storing it.

☐ Let the ashes cool completely before emptying the ash catcher into a metal can.

☐ When grilling on a windy day, take precautions to protect the flame.

FOOD SAFETY

Here are a few guidelines for food safety while cooking outdoors:

☐ Most of us grill in warm weather, so take precautions to keep food at safe temperatures. Never let uncooked food sit for more than 1 hour at room temperature.

☐ Use a separate platter to transport raw food, to avoid cross-contamination.

☐ If you plan to baste meat or poultry with the same mixture you used to marinate it, reserve a small portion of the marinade for basting before you pour the remainder over raw food; alternatively, boil the marinade for 2 minutes before using it for basting. Once you have used a marinade, discard it.

☐ Wash basting brushes that touched raw food before using them on grilled foods.

☐ Wash thermometers after you insert them in foods, whether raw or fully cooked.

☐ Take the internal temperatures of meat, poultry, or fish; cook to a safe temperature.

☐ Promptly refrigerate grilled foods that have cooled and are leftovers.

GRILL TOOLS

It goes without saying that if you like to grill, you probably like grill gear. Having long-handled tools dangling from the hooks at the front of the grill is handy, fun, and empowering. Within easy reach, you have a grill brush, a spatula, a silicone basting brush, and tongs—the essentials. This list consists of both must-have items and other useful but optional tools. At the end, I have included some fun and even a few wacky tools that grill lovers might want to own. The list of gear for barbecuing is much longer and would include disposable drip pans, smoker boxes, basting mops, and lots more. I've kept this list to just what's needed for weeknight grilling.

MUST-HAVE TOOLS

CHIMNEY STARTER AND ELECTRIC STARTER For charcoal grilling only. These two tools are the safest, most efficient and eco-friendly ways to start a fire for a charcoal grill, dispensing fully with nasty lighter fluid. A chimney starter is essentially a large steel can with vent holes in the bottom and a few up the sides, plus a sturdy heatproof handle. You crumple newspaper into the bottom of the can and pour charcoal on top. Light a match to the paper, and the coals begin to blaze. When the coals are hot, you simply dump them into the grill. Chimney starters come in different sizes; buy one that holds enough charcoal to cover the charcoal grate of your grill in a single full layer (see page 20 for a detailed discussion).

Electric starters typically have an oval heating coil with a heatproof handle and a long electrical cord. You'll need an electrical outlet near the grill. You plug in the starter and nest the coil under a layer of charcoal. After about 20 minutes, the majority of the coals will be blazing and covered with gray ash. Whether you use an electric starter or chimney starter, you need to find a safe, heatproof place away from children and pets to let the starter cool down.

GRILL BRUSH A long-handled grill brush for cleaning the grill grate before and after cooking is critical to successful grilling. The best grill brushes have a wooden handle, replaceable brass bristles, and a stainless-steel scraper. Actually, I own two grill brushes—the one I just described, plus a triangular brush with steel bristles along the bottom. It does a good job of getting between the bars of the grate.

TONGS My favorite grill tool is a good pair of tongs, essential for turning food and for moving around the coals. Grill tongs should be long, strong, made of stainless steel, and ideally spring-loaded. I like tongs that lock in a closed position for easy storage. OXO makes tongs that have comfortable cushioned, nonslip handles, plus they are rounded, rather than serrated, at the top. Buy tongs 16 inches long for moving around the coals, and 12- to 14-inch tongs for turning the food.

INSTANT-READ THERMOMETER   This small-dial, thin-shaft thermometer is the most accurate way to judge the doneness of most grilled meats, poultry, and fish. You must not leave the thermometer in the food, however. Instead, you insert it, get an "instant read," and then out it comes. Also, be sure that it doesn't touch bone, which can skew the reading. For safety and sanitation, always wash the thermometer before reinserting it in any food. I prefer an analog thermometer to a digital one, as the readings on the digital models seem to jump around from one temperature to another.

BASTING BRUSHES   Brushes are essential, and the new silicone-bristled ones are superb. They won't burn and they are much easier to clean than nylon-bristled brushes. I have a long-handled one for basting and a short-handled one for brushing oil or butter on foods before they go on the grill.

SPATULAS   A long-handled metal spatula is necessary for flipping burgers, turning meats, supporting delicate vegetables, and turning wide items like quesadillas. Buy one that has a long, wide, sturdy blade. For turning fish, I prefer to use a fish spatula, which has a wide, thin, slotted blade with a tapered front edge, allowing you to get under the delicate fillet with maximum flexibility.

GRILL MITTS   A pair of well-insulated, heavy-duty, long-down-the-arm mitts will keep your hands and forearms protected. I wear them when I am dumping coals from the chimney starter into the grill, reaching to the back of the grill, or lifting a pizza pan off the grate. I like the long synthetic mitts made by Kitchen Grips (available at retail kitchenware stores) which are heat-resistant to 500°F. Silicone mitts work well, too; buy ones that allow a good grip.

SKEWERS   Grilling satay and kebabs requires skewers. There are several types available, some better than others, some cheaper than others. Most readily available and the cheapest to use are round bamboo skewers sold in varying lengths. These skewers, as well as all other bamboo or other wooden skewers, need to be soaked for at least 15 minutes before use so they don't burn on the grill. A clever idea is to soak the skewers when you buy them, shake off the water, and store them in a lock-top plastic bag in the freezer. They are ready to use when you need them, no soaking required.

Flat bamboo skewers, even double-pronged ones, prevent foods from spinning as you turn them on the grill. Flat-edged metal skewers or U-shaped double skewers are a permanent solution, as they are reusable, don't burn, and keep the food from spinning. Buy two lengths—shorter 7-inch ones and longer 10-inch ones for all your skewer needs. Finally, seasoned skewers are available at kitchenware shops and gourmet grocery stores. These are flat, wooden skewers that have been infused with different flavor profiles, such as Thai coconut lime. Instead of marinating foods, you thread them onto seasoned skewers, which impart flavor to them from within. Personally, I prefer traditional marinating techniques and find these skewers too expensive at almost a dollar each.

Skewers can also be made out of fresh ingredients, such as rosemary sprigs, sturdy thyme branches, lemongrass stalks, and even strips of sugarcane. These strike me as ambitious to use for weeknight grilling, but keep them in mind for entertaining and relaxed weekend grilling.

SPRAY BOTTLE   I keep a plastic spray bottle filled with water near the grill in case of flare-ups. Buy a plastic bottle at the hardware store and label it "water for the grill," distinguishing it from other bottles that might have, say, bleach solution in them!

OPTIONAL BUT HANDY TOOLS

REMOTE THERMOMETER   This thermometer is made up of a probe with a thin wire connected to a transmitter. You insert the probe into the food, put the transmitter on a counter next to the grill (or conventional oven), and program the transmitter with the desired temperature. The newest versions have a transmitter and wireless remote, so you can walk up to 120 feet away and the pager will beep when the food is done. These thermometers are cool, but Internet reviews have been mixed. If you like reading manuals and figuring out how to program gadgets, this tool is for you.

GRILL BASKETS AND GRIDS   I haven't included a recipe for grilling a whole fish or whole fish fillet in this book (other than on a wood plank), but I often use a hinged, fish-shaped grill basket when I do grill them. It is the perfect tool for the task because the fish is securely contained, it can sit above the grill grate so the skin doesn't stick, and it can be easily turned. A grill grid keeps small foods, such as figs, shrimp, scallops, onion slices, and even aspara-gus, from falling through the grate. I don't like the look of food that has been grilled on a perforated metal plate, and I find hinged grill baskets cumbersome and a nuisance to clean. But I tried a nonstick wire grilling grid with loop handles designed by grilling guru Steven Raichlen, and it is the best I have found. I load the grid with food, place it directly on the grate, and turn the food without fear of losing it through the wires. The grid is relatively inexpensive, plus it's easy to clean and store.

PIZZA STONE   If you love the really crisp crust your pizzas get using the high heat (500° to 600°F) of a covered grill, then consider investing in a PizzaGrill made by VillaWare (available at Williams-Sonoma or online at amazon.com). The unique design features a large pizza stone resting inside a raised stainless-steel frame with a built-in thermometer and a back-splash that keeps your pizza from slipping off the stone. The stone is raised off the grill grate, which permits air circulation and prevents the bottom of the crust from burning. If you use the PizzaGrill, you must build your pizza on a peel or an inverted baking sheet, from which you can slide it onto the hot stone. The stone can also be used in a conventional oven.

FUN AND WACKY GEAR

FOR BEER-CAN CHICKEN ENTHUSIASTS Because it takes almost an hour for the chicken perched on a beer can to cook, I consider beer-can chicken a grilling method better reserved for weekend fun. But a clever tool on the market that replaces the tipsy beer can deserves a mention here. It is called the Turkey Cannon, made by Camp Chef (see Sources, page 220), and it won the Best Barbecue Accessory award at the Hearth, Patio & Barbecue Association's national exposition in 2006. An open steel frame supports an 8- or 10-inch-long steel tube that rises from the frame in a somewhat, how should I say this, erect position. Liquid, such as beer, wine, or even a garlic-and-herb-infused marinade, is poured into the tube, and the chicken or turkey is supported by inserting the tube into the bird's breast cavity. The clever design allows the bird to grill-roast above the grill grate at an angle that encourages air to flow freely around it. It cooks from the outside as well as from the inside, because heat and moisture are forced into the cavity of the bird.

THE GRILLSLINGER FOR HOLDING TOOLS This is the inspiration of a couple of guys from New Zealand. Like the hip-hugging tool belt that electricians and framers use, the Grillslinger fits around your waist, supposedly, and you can dangle your grill tools in its various pockets. (It comes with several grill tools, all with handles that are too short.) I tried to make the circumference as small as possible, but the belt still fell off my hips—it's truly meant for guys. To me, this falls into the "not necessary, slightly wacky" grill-tool category. That said, this belt would be handy for anyone short on counter space at the grill. The Grillslinger comes with a storage bag, so you can easily take it if you're going car camping or to the beach and will be trying to use a portable grill with limited space for holding tools. The Grillslinger is available at grillslinger.com.

GRILLIN' IN THE DARK Without a patio light, consider a grill light that clamps on the side of the grill. They are available as either plug-in or battery-operated lights.

SPECIALTY GRILL BASKETS Grill-gear geeks might want to go crazy and buy a grill basket for every possible food item: corn baskets, shish kebab baskets, garlic bread rack, and on and on. But who wants to clean all those baskets, and where do you store them? The Steven Raichlen wire grid (see facing page) works fine for all of these foods. Save your money and buy the best grill you can afford!

THE GRILL PANTRY

EVERY GRILL MASTER has a pantry and a refrigerator full of lip-buzzing dry rubs, infused oils, heady barbecue sauces, exotic pastes, flavor-packed glazes, mop sauces, basting sauces, and wet rubs. You can hardly tell whether the refrigerator shelves are filled with secret sauces or chemistry experiments—or maybe one and the same! Many of these intriguing combinations lend themselves to what I call weekend-warrior grilling, the relaxed time at week's end when you marinate a tough cut of meat overnight and then smoke-grill it over a low fire for five hours until it's meltingly tender. Or, you cover a rack of pork ribs with your signature dry rub and leave it in a smoker pit for at least twelve hours—a recipe that wins you first place in the local barbecue cook-off. I'm a fan, a big fan, of weekend marathon grilling and partying. But it's not the type of grilling that a stretched-thin parent like me can pull off on a weeknight. I need a pantry of simple rubs and pastes that I either make myself or buy at the store, plus a repertoire of easy recipes that call for them.

Building a pantry for weeknight grilling is all about flavor and convenience. In this chapter, you'll find some of my favorite rubs, pastes, and sauces, preparations that I use over and over again. For instance, the Grill Every Day Spice Rub (page 31) is mixed into ground buffalo for Buffalo Burgers with Pepper Jack Cheese (page 51), patted onto pork for Chili-Rubbed Pork Tenderloin with Nectarine Salsa (page 68), suggested as a rub for planked salmon (page 86), slathered on shrimp for Chili-Rubbed Shrimp with Soft Tacos and Salsa (page 101), and massaged into chicken for Chili-Rubbed Chicken Thighs with Smashed Grilled Potatoes and Mole Sauce (page 122). It's versatile and guaranteed to jump-start any backyard grill fest. As I suggest in the recipe, make a big batch of the rub over the weekend when you have time, and keep it on the pantry shelf for rushed weeknight meals. That's true for almost all the recipes in this chapter, which makes them ideal for the busy cook.

To expand my pantry further and bring even more global flavors to the grill, I walk the aisles of ethnic markets and gourmet grocery stores in search of fragrant rubs, electrifying sauces, piquant pastes, and interesting infused oils to pair with foods for the grill. A number of recipes in the book use my favorite purchased sauces and rubs, and I include others I like in Sources on page 220.

Grill Every Day Spice Rub

This is my favorite big-flavored spice blend, guaranteed to ignite great taste when rubbed on shrimp, scallops, chicken, beef, lamb, buffalo, or pork. This recipe yields just over a cup; I tend to triple it, so I have extra rub on my pantry shelf when I need it. I make the big batch on a weekend when I have extra time, and then—voilà—it's there when I want it on a time-strapped weeknight.

[MAKES ABOUT 1¼ CUPS]

¼	CUP KOSHER OR SEA SALT
2	TABLESPOONS COARSELY GROUND PEPPER
1	TABLESPOON GROUND CORIANDER
3	TABLESPOONS GROUND CUMIN
2	TABLESPOONS SWEET PAPRIKA
2	TABLESPOONS DRIED THYME, CRUSHED
2	TABLESPOONS CHILI POWDER
¼	CUP PACKED DARK BROWN SUGAR
2	TEASPOONS GROUND CINNAMON

In a small bowl, combine the salt, pepper, coriander, cumin, paprika, thyme, chili powder, sugar, and cinnamon. Stir well to blend. Use immediately, or transfer to a jar with a tight-fitting lid and store away from heat and light for up to 6 months.

Latin Spice Rub

I like to keep this rub on hand for seasoning pork, chicken, and flank steak. The recipe makes only a small quantity—enough to rub 2 pork tenderloins, 4 pork chops, or about 1 pound of flank steak—so make extra for your pantry shelf.

[MAKES ABOUT ¼ CUP]

1	TABLESPOON PACKED DARK BROWN SUGAR
1½	TEASPOONS KOSHER OR SEA SALT
1½	TEASPOONS FRESHLY GROUND PEPPER
1½	TEASPOONS GROUND GINGER
1½	TEASPOONS GROUND CUMIN
½	TEASPOON CAYENNE PEPPER

In a small bowl, combine the sugar, salt, pepper, ginger, cumin, and cayenne pepper. Stir well to blend. Use immediately, or transfer to a jar with a tight-fitting lid and store away from heat and light for up to 6 months.

Espresso-Cardamom Rub

When I was teaching grilling techniques with colleagues Rick Rodgers and David Garrido at a dude ranch in Arizona, David made a grilled cowboy steak (featured on page 46) that he seasoned with finely ground coffee, ground chile, and salt. The ground coffee caramelized the steak, giving it a rich flavor and color. I expanded on his idea and created this rub for beef, pork, and chicken thighs and legs.

[MAKES ABOUT 1 CUP]

¼	CUP FINELY GROUND ESPRESSO-ROAST COFFEE
¼	CUP KOSHER OR SEA SALT
¼	CUP PACKED DARK BROWN SUGAR
3	TABLESPOONS HOT PAPRIKA
1	TABLESPOON GROUND CARDAMOM
1	TABLESPOON GROUND GINGER
2	TEASPOONS GARLIC POWDER

In a small bowl, combine the coffee, salt, sugar, paprika, cardamom, ginger, and garlic powder. Stir well to blend. Use immediately, or transfer to a jar with a tight-fitting lid and store away from heat and light for up to 1 month.

Jerk Paste

Jamaicans know how to bring spice and fiery flavors to their wood pits. Although many variations on jerk paste exist, it usually consists of chiles, onions, ginger, garlic, cilantro, allspice, and thyme. Authentic jerk paste has a list of ingredients a mile long and an unbelievable amount of Scotch bonnet chiles. I've trimmed the list and cut the quantity of chiles to make this as easy as possible for the weeknight griller. Because jerk paste has a long shelf life, I recommend making the recipe on the weekend as a leisure-cooking activity, and then firing up your grill and your taste buds for a weeknight meal. Jerk paste is sensational on pork, chicken, fish fillets, or shrimp.

2 TO 4	SCOTCH BONNET OR HABANERO CHILES, INCLUDING SEEDS, QUARTERED (SEE COOK'S NOTE)
1	SMALL YELLOW ONION, QUARTERED
3	GREEN ONIONS, INCLUDING GREEN TOPS, CUT INTO 1-INCH LENGTHS
4	QUARTER-SIZED SLICES PEELED FRESH GINGER
3	CLOVES GARLIC
½	CUP PACKED COARSELY CHOPPED FRESH CILANTRO
¼	CUP PACKED DARK BROWN SUGAR
2	TABLESPOONS KOSHER OR SEA SALT
1	TABLESPOON GROUND ALLSPICE
1	TABLESPOON DRIED THYME
1	TABLESPOON COARSELY GROUND PEPPER
¼	CUP FRESH LIME JUICE
¼	CUP SOY SAUCE
2	TABLESPOONS VEGETABLE OIL

[MAKES ABOUT 1¾ CUPS]

In a food processor fitted with the metal blade, combine the chiles, yellow onion, green onions, ginger, garlic, and cilantro and process until finely minced. Add the sugar, salt, allspice, thyme, and pepper and process to combine. Add the lime juice, soy sauce, and oil and process until a paste forms. Use immediately, or transfer to a jar with a tight-fitting lid and refrigerate for up to 3 months.

 COOK'S NOTE Get yourself some disposable surgical gloves at the pharmacy and wear them when you work with chiles. They will keep the caustic compound (capsaicin) that is naturally present in chiles from irritating your skin.

Moroccan Pesto

This is my version of *charmoula*, a traditional Moroccan marinade. Although it can be used to marinate meats and poultry, I serve it as a sauce to accompany grilled lamb and chicken. This pesto is garlicky and tart and packed with the heady flavor of cilantro, making it the perfect partner.

[MAKES ABOUT ½ CUP]

⅓ CUP COARSELY CHOPPED FRESH CILANTRO
2 TABLESPOONS COARSELY CHOPPED FRESH FLAT-LEAF PARSLEY
2 LARGE CLOVES GARLIC
1 TEASPOON GROUND CUMIN
½ TEASPOON KOSHER OR SEA SALT
¼ TEASPOON CAYENNE PEPPER
3 TABLESPOONS FRESH LEMON JUICE
¼ CUP EXTRA-VIRGIN OLIVE OIL

In a food processor fitted with the metal blade, combine the cilantro, parsley, garlic, cumin, salt, and cayenne pepper and process until the herbs and garlic are finely chopped. With the machine running, pour the lemon juice and olive oil through the feed tube and process until the sauce is combined. Use immediately, or transfer to a jar with a tight-fitting lid and refrigerate for up to 3 days.

Lemongrass Paste

This is a wonderful paste for grilling, lending an Asian flair to meats and tofu. I use it for Lemongrass-Grilled Lamb Loin Chops (page 61) and Lemongrass-Grilled Tofu with Thai Peanut Sauce (page 164). Don't stop there, though. It's terrific on shrimp, smeared over pork chops or pork tenderloin, and rubbed on beef skewers.

I have made this paste in a mini-chop food processor, but because it is so fibrous, I prefer to mince the lemongrass by hand with a sharp chef's knife. If you frequent Asian markets, look for finely minced lemongrass in the freezer compartment and keep some on hand. It is imported from Vietnam and comes in clear plastic containers.

[MAKES ABOUT ½ CUP]

2   STALKS LEMONGRASS
2   SHALLOTS, FINELY MINCED
¼   CUP SUGAR
3   TABLESPOONS VEGETABLE OIL
2   TEASPOONS FISH SAUCE
2   TEASPOONS RED PEPPER FLAKES

Cut off and discard the dried grasslike top half of the lemongrass. Trim the base of the bulb end and then remove and discard the tough outer leaves. Using only the white and light green parts, cut in half lengthwise, and then cut crosswise to mince finely.

In a small bowl, combine the lemongrass, shallots, sugar, vegetable oil, fish sauce, and red pepper flakes. Stir well to blend. Use immediately, or transfer to a jar with a tight-fitting lid and refrigerate for up to 3 days or freeze for up to 2 months.

Hoisin-Ginger Basting Sauce

Combine just six classic Asian ingredients and watch them create a thousand layers of sweet, smoky, pungent flavors. This versatile sauce is delicious on chicken, pork, and tofu.

[MAKES ABOUT 1¼ CUPS]

½	CUP HOISIN SAUCE
¼	CUP PLUM SAUCE
¼	CUP LOW-SODIUM SOY SAUCE
2	TABLESPOONS ASIAN SESAME OIL
1	TABLESPOON PEELED AND MINCED FRESH GINGER
1	LARGE CLOVE GARLIC, MINCED
1	TEASPOON RED PEPPER FLAKES

In a small bowl, combine the hoisin sauce, plum sauce, soy sauce, sesame oil, ginger, garlic, and red pepper flakes. Stir well to blend. Use immediately, or transfer to a jar with a tight-fitting lid and refrigerate for up to 1 month.

BEEF, BUFFALO + LAMB

* FLANK STEAK THINLY SLICED OVER ARUGULA WITH GARLIC AND LEMON OIL 41
* FLANK STEAK WITH A HORSERADISH, PARSLEY, AND CROUTON SALAD 42
* HOISIN-GRILLED FLANK STEAK 43
* TUSCAN-STYLE PORTERHOUSE STEAK WITH CAPERS, OLIVES, AND RED BELL PEPPERS 44
* COWBOY-GRILLED RIB-EYE STEAK 46
* KANSAS CITY STRIP STEAK PERFECTION 47
* SKIRT STEAK, ARGENTINE STYLE 48
* SKIRT STEAK AND GRILLED FINGERLING POTATOES WITH CRUMBLED BLUE CHEESE SAUCE 49
* HANGER STEAKS WITH CHILE-RUBBED GRILLED ONIONS 50
* BUFFALO BURGERS WITH PEPPER JACK CHEESE 51
* THE BIG BEEF BURGER STUFFED WITH BLUE CHEESE 52
* CHAR-GRILLED LAMB BURGERS WITH GARLIC-AND-MINT YOGURT SAUCE 54
* LAMB STEAKS WITH *HERBES DE PROVENCE* SPICE RUB 56
* MUSTARD-AND-ROSEMARY-CRUSTED LAMB STEAKS 57
* CUMIN-RUBBED LAMB CHOPS WITH MOROCCAN PESTO SAUCE 58
* ROSEMARY-AND-GARLIC-CRUSTED LAMB CHOPS 60
* LEMONGRASS-GRILLED LAMB LOIN CHOPS 61

BEEF, BUFFALO, AND LAMB ON THE GRILL

Mastering meat on the grill is all about getting a good sear on the outside while keeping the inside juicy, tender, and rare to medium-rare. Different techniques are involved, depending on the cut and thickness. You'll quickly find out that one important technique to master is the two-zone fire (see page 21), which allows you to sear the meat over high heat and then move it to a cooler zone to finish cooking. If you are a novice and want to start out with the easiest meat to grill, I suggest you try flank steak. It's a sturdy cut that adapts well to different marinades, pastes, and dry rubs. Plus, trimmed properly, flank steak has little fat, so flare-ups are minimized. Here are some other basic guidelines and techniques that will bring you grilling success when meat is on the menu.

FIRST, start with a clean, hot, well-oiled grill surface. You want to get a good sear on the meat, so even small bits of charred food left on the grate will interfere with achieving an even sear with well-etched grill marks. Preheat the grill; brush the grate so it's clean, clean, clean; and oil the grate thoroughly so it's well coated and slick.

SECOND, never put a cold piece of meat on the grill. Remove the meat from the refrigerator 20 to 30 minutes prior to grilling. If there is any residual moisture on it, blot it dry with paper towels before marinating or using a dry rub.

THIRD, use the right tools for turning the meat. For steaks and chops, I always use tongs, never a two-pronged fork, to move or turn the meat, because a fork will pierce it, allowing the juices to run out.

FOURTH, the cooking times provided are just guidelines. Your best bet for a juicy rare or medium-rare piece of meat is to use an instant-read thermometer. Remember that the meat will continue to cook after it comes off the grill, rising in temperature 3 to 6 degrees, so if you want a medium-rare steak, take it off the grill when it tests just below medium-rare, and by the time it rests, it will be perfect. Experimentation and practice will help you get the result you want.

FINALLY, meat needs to rest when it comes off the grill. During cooking, the heat drives the juices into the cells and into the center of the meat. If you cut meat the moment you take if off the grill, the juices will spill out on the carving board and the meat will be less tender. If you allow the meat to rest for 5 minutes before you cut into it, the juices will redistribute themselves evenly throughout the meat, leaving it juicy and tender when sliced.

Flank Steak Thinly Sliced over Arugula with Garlic and Lemon Oil

I told my dear friend and colleague Cathy Whims, co-owner of Portland's renowned restaurant Nostrana, that I was "stealing her recipe" after I ate this dish at her restaurant. The simplicity of the preparation was obvious, yet the overlay of flavors was complex and memorable. It's a winner! Grill an extra flank steak and reserve it for making Grilled Flank Steak Salad with Grilled New Potatoes and *Chimichurri* (page 199) on another night.

[SERVES 4]

1   FLANK STEAK, 1¼ TO 1½ POUNDS, TRIMMED OF FAT
2   TABLESPOONS EXTRA-VIRGIN OLIVE OIL
1   TEASPOON MINCED GARLIC
KOSHER OR SEA SALT
FRESHLY GROUND PEPPER
6   OUNCES BABY ARUGULA LEAVES
2¼ CUPS LEMON-INFUSED EXTRA-VIRGIN OLIVE OIL (SEE COOK'S NOTE)
FLEUR DE SEL OR OTHER FINISHING SALT FOR SPRINKLING

Prepare a hot fire in a charcoal grill or preheat a gas grill on high.

Remove the flank steak from the refrigerator 20 to 30 minutes before grilling and place it on a large, rimmed baking sheet. In a small bowl, combine the 2 tablespoons olive oil and the garlic. Rub the steak on both sides with the mixture and season with salt and pepper.

Oil the grill grate. Place the flank steak directly over the hot fire. Cover the grill and sear the steak on one side, 4 minutes for rare or 6 minutes for medium-rare. Turn, re-cover, and cook for 4 minutes more, or until an instant-read thermometer registers 120°F for rare or 130° to 135°F for medium-rare.

Transfer the steak to a carving board and let rest for 5 minutes. Cut the meat across the grain into ¼-inch-thick slices. Scatter an equal amount of arugula on each dinner plate. Arrange overlapping slices of steak over the greens and spoon any accumulated juices over the top. Drizzle 1 tablespoon of the lemon olive oil over each portion of steak and sprinkle with *fleur de sel*. Serve immediately.

COOK'S NOTE Citrus-infused extra-virgin olive oils add big flavor to simply prepared foods, such as grilled steak, chicken, and vegetables, making the oils a staple in my grilling pantry. I buy them at specialty-foods stores, natural-foods stores, and Trader Joe's.

Flank Steak with a Horseradish, Parsley, and Crouton Salad

A big-flavored, crunchy bread salad is what makes this main dish so fabulous. Simply grilled flank steak, seasoned with a touch of garlic, is the backdrop for a parsley and crouton salad tossed with a pleasantly assertive mustard and horseradish vinaigrette. Plan ahead and have some day-old bread, either a crusty baguette or an artisanal country-style loaf, on hand for making croutons. Store-bought croutons are too dry for this salad; the bread needs to be toasted but still a little chewy at the center.

1	FLANK STEAK, 1¼ TO 1½ POUNDS, TRIMMED OF FAT
2	TABLESPOONS EXTRA-VIRGIN OLIVE OIL
1	TEASPOON MINCED GARLIC
	KOSHER OR SEA SALT
	FRESHLY GROUND PEPPER

[SERVES 4]

½	CUP EXTRA-VIRGIN OLIVE OIL
1½	TABLESPOONS FRESH LEMON JUICE
1½	TABLESPOONS COARSE-GRAIN MUSTARD
1½	TABLESPOONS PREPARED HORSERADISH
1	TEASPOON FRESHLY GROUND PEPPER
½	TEASPOON KOSHER OR SEA SALT
½	TEASPOON SUGAR
2	TABLESPOONS CAPERS, RINSED AND DRAINED
3	CUPS ¾-INCH-CUBED DAY-OLD BAGUETTE OR ARTISANAL BREAD, LIGHTLY TOASTED
2	CUPS LOOSELY PACKED FRESH FLAT-LEAF PARSLEY LEAVES
1	CUP BABY ARUGULA LEAVES

SALAD

Prepare a hot fire in a charcoal grill or preheat a gas grill on high.

Remove the flank steak from the refrigerator 20 to 30 minutes before grilling and place it on a large, rimmed baking sheet. In a small bowl, combine the 2 tablespoons olive oil and the garlic. Rub the steak on both sides with the mixture and season with salt and pepper.

While the grill is heating, make the salad: In a large bowl, whisk together the ½ cup olive oil, lemon juice, mustard, horseradish, pepper, salt, and sugar. Stir in the capers and set aside.

Oil the grill grate. Place the flank steak directly over the hot fire. Cover the grill and sear the steak on one side, 4 minutes for rare or 6 minutes for medium-rare. Turn, re-cover, and cook for 4 minutes more, or until an instant-read thermometer registers 120°F for rare or 130° to 135°F for medium-rare. Transfer the steak to a carving board and let rest for 5 minutes.

While the steak is resting, toss the salad. Give the dressing a last-minute stir, then add the bread cubes, parsley, and arugula to the bowl and toss gently to mix.

Cut the meat across the grain into $^1/_4$-inch-thick slices. Divide the slices evenly among warmed dinner plates and spoon any accumulated juices over the top. Arrange a mound of salad to the side of the steak or on top of the slices. Serve immediately.

Hoisin-Grilled Flank Steak

For a weeknight meal, flank steak has everything going for it: it's versatile, it's relatively inexpensive, and it's quick to grill. I've streamlined what could be a more elaborate marinade, keeping the essence of an Asian-flavored steak without a long list of ingredients. Because the marinade is sweet, keep an eye on the steak and watch the timing to ensure a nice sear with dark grill marks but no charring. Start the steak directly over the hot coals and then move it to the cooler side of the grill for both a great sear and the ideal degree of doneness.

[SERVES 4]

1   FLANK STEAK, 1¼ TO 1½ POUNDS, TRIMMED OF FAT
¼   CUP HOISIN SAUCE
2   TABLESPOONS PLUM SAUCE
2   TEASPOONS MINCED GARLIC
1   TEASPOON RED PEPPER FLAKES

Prepare a hot fire in a charcoal grill or preheat a gas grill on high.

Remove the flank steak from the refrigerator 20 to 30 minutes before grilling and place it on a large, rimmed baking sheet. In a small bowl, stir together the hoisin and plum sauces, garlic, and red pepper flakes. Liberally rub the steak on both sides with the mixture.

To create a cool zone, bank the coals to one side of the grill or turn off one of the burners. Oil the grill grate. Place the flank steak directly over the hot fire. Cover the grill and sear the steak on one side for 3 to 4 minutes. Turn, re-cover, and cook for 3 minutes more. Move the flank steak to the cooler part of the grill, cover, and grill for about 4 minutes longer, or until an instant-read thermometer registers 120°F for rare or 130° to 135°F for medium-rare.

Transfer the steak to a carving board and let rest for 5 minutes. Cut the meat across the grain into $^1/_4$-inch-thick slices. Divide the slices evenly among warmed dinner plates and spoon any accumulated juices over the top. Serve immediately.

Tuscan-Style Porterhouse Steak
with Capers, Olives, and Red Bell Peppers

When what you want is a hunky steak to grill, go for a porterhouse, which is really two steaks in one. It has both a firm, meaty strip steak and a tenderloin attached to the bone. Steak lovers are partial to meat cooked on the bone for the beefiest flavor (and also because gnawing on the seared bones has serious appeal). If you think of grilled steak as very American, one trip to Tuscany will set you straight. The Tuscans have mastered steak with the classic *bistecca alla fiorentina*, a porterhouse grilled and served on a big wood board, drizzled with peppery Tuscan olive oil and a squeeze of lemon juice, and sprinkled with coarse sea salt. This recipe embellishes Tuscany's basic preparation with a colorful bell pepper topping.

[SERVES 4]

2	PORTERHOUSE STEAKS, 1½ INCHES THICK (ABOUT 1½ POUNDS EACH)
1	TABLESPOON EXTRA-VIRGIN OLIVE OIL; PLUS MORE FOR THE RUB
	KOSHER OR SEA SALT
¼	TEASPOON FRESHLY GROUND PEPPER; PLUS MORE FOR SEASONING
3	RED BELL PEPPERS, QUARTERED, SEEDED, AND DERIBBED
1	CUP CERIGNOLA OR SICILIAN GREEN OLIVES, PITTED AND HALVED
¼	CUP CAPERS, RINSED AND DRAINED
1	TABLESPOON MINCED FRESH FLAT-LEAF PARSLEY

Prepare a hot fire in a charcoal grill or preheat a gas grill on high.

Remove the steaks from the refrigerator 20 to 30 minutes before grilling and place them on a large, rimmed baking sheet. Rub the steaks on both sides with olive oil. Liberally season the steaks on both sides with salt and pepper.

Place the bell peppers in a bowl and toss with just enough olive oil to coat them lightly. In another bowl, combine the olives, capers, parsley, and ¼ teaspoon freshly ground pepper. Set aside.

Oil the grill grate. Place the peppers directly over the hot fire. Cover the grill and cook, turning once, until dark brown grill marks appear and the peppers are crisp-tender, 4 to 5 minutes. Transfer the peppers to a cutting board.

Oil the grill grate again and place the steaks directly over the hot fire. Grill the steaks on one side, 5 minutes for rare or 6 minutes for medium-rare. Turn and cook for 5 minutes more, or until an instant-read thermometer registers 120°F for rare or 130° to 135°F for medium-rare. Transfer the steaks to a carving board and let rest for 5 minutes. >>

Tuscan-Style Porterhouse Steak with Capers, Olives, and Red Bell Peppers
(*continued*)

While the steaks are resting, cut the grilled peppers lengthwise into $^1/_2$-inch-wide strips and add to the bowl with the olives. Add 1 tablespoon olive oil and toss gently to combine.

Using a sharp knife, cut along the bone of each steak, separating it from the meat. Cut the meat across the grain into $^1/_2$-inch-thick slices. Arrange overlapping slices of steak on warmed dinner plates or a platter, and spoon the bell pepper mixture over the top. Serve immediately.

Cowboy-Grilled Rib-Eye Steak

Steak the way the cowboys made it! Without a spice rack on the trail, those boys got inventive and used ground coffee and dried chiles to season their steaks. They were on to somethin'. This is steak the way it's meant to be: stripped down to its primal essence—juicy, rare, and tender. Cowboys wouldn't have had *fleur de sel* at the campfire, unless they were French cowboys, but if they had had it, they sure would have liked it. Use coffee that has been either ground for espresso or ground for a drip pot. Coffee ground for a French press is too gritty for rubbing on steaks.

[SERVES 4]

4   RIB-EYE STEAKS, 1½ INCHES THICK (ABOUT 10 OUNCES EACH)
EXTRA-VIRGIN OLIVE OIL
2   TABLESPOONS FINELY GROUND DARK-ROAST COFFEE
GROUND CHIPOTLE CHILE FOR DUSTING
FLEUR DE SEL OR OTHER FINISHING SALT FOR SPRINKLING

Prepare a hot fire in a charcoal grill or preheat a gas grill on high.

Remove the steaks from the refrigerator 20 to 30 minutes before grilling and place them on a large, rimmed baking sheet. Rub the steaks on both sides with olive oil. Liberally season the steaks on both sides with the coffee and chile, lightly pressing the seasonings into the meat.

Oil the grill grate. Place the steaks directly over the hot fire. Grill the steaks on one side, 4 minutes for rare or 6 minutes for medium-rare. Turn and cook for 4 minutes more, or until an instant-read thermometer registers 120°F for rare or 130° to 135°F for medium-rare.

Remove the steaks from the grill and let rest for 5 minutes. Sprinkle the steaks generously with *fleur de sel* just before serving.

Kansas City Strip Steak Perfection

Biases prevail here. My husband is from Kansas City, Missouri, where beef is taken seriously and dry-aged, grain-fed beef delivers the best marbling. In fact, many folks drive out of their way to buy beef from McGonigle's Market in Kansas City (see Sources, page 220). Since we only get to Kansas City once or twice a year, we have our steaks express-shipped to us. This may seem like an extravagant and expensive proposition, but in comparison to the "best" steaks we can buy in the Northwest, there is no competition. I laugh every time I open a box of the steaks, which includes the following directions: "You were sent a really good piece of meat. Your job is to not screw it up!" For me, two critical rules apply for the perfect steak: use only minimal seasonings so as not to mask the flavor of the beef, and never ruin a good steak with steak sauce!

[SERVES 4]

4   STRIP STEAKS, 1 INCH THICK (ABOUT 12 OUNCES EACH)
EXTRA-VIRGIN OLIVE OIL
KOSHER OR SEA SALT
FRESHLY GROUND PEPPER

Prepare a hot fire in a charcoal grill or preheat a gas grill on high.

Remove the steaks from the refrigerator 20 to 30 minutes before grilling and place them on a large, rimmed baking sheet. Rub the steaks on both sides with olive oil. Liberally season the steaks on both sides with salt and pepper.

Oil the grill grate. Place the steaks directly over the hot fire. Grill the steaks on one side, 4 minutes for rare or 6 minutes for medium-rare. Turn and cook for 4 minutes more, or until an instant-read thermometer registers 120°F for rare or 130° to 135°F for medium-rare.

Remove the steaks from the grill and let rest for 5 minutes before serving.

Skirt Steak, Argentine Style

Full-flavored, inexpensive skirt steak is great for grilling. It can measure more than a foot long and is quite thin, so searing it quickly over high heat is best. If it seems too unwieldy to manage, cut it in half crosswise; the shorter pieces are easier to grill. For this recipe, I pair skirt steak with *chimichurri*, a classic garlicky herb sauce of Argentina, a country famous for its beef. The sauce is a cinch to make with a food processor. Save some hand chopping and mince the garlic for the steaks in the processor before you make the sauce.

[SERVES 4]

2 TO 2½ POUNDS SKIRT STEAK, TRIMMED OF EXCESS FAT
2 TABLESPOONS EXTRA-VIRGIN OLIVE OIL
2 LARGE CLOVES GARLIC, MINCED
KOSHER OR SEA SALT
FRESHLY GROUND PEPPER

CHIMICHURRI

2 LARGE CLOVES GARLIC
1 TEASPOON RED PEPPER FLAKES
½ TEASPOON GROUND CUMIN
½ TEASPOON KOSHER OR SEA SALT
½ TEASPOON SUGAR
1 CUP PACKED FRESH FLAT-LEAF PARSLEY LEAVES
¼ CUP FRESH LEMON JUICE
½ CUP EXTRA-VIRGIN OLIVE OIL

Prepare a hot fire in a charcoal grill or preheat a gas grill on high.

Remove the steaks from the refrigerator 20 to 30 minutes before grilling and place them on a large, rimmed baking sheet. In a small bowl, combine the 2 tablespoons olive oil and the garlic. Rub the steaks on both sides with the mixture. Lightly season the steaks on both sides with salt and pepper.

While the grill is heating, make the *chimichurri*: In a food processor fitted with the metal blade, combine the garlic, red pepper flakes, cumin, ½ teaspoon salt, and sugar and process until the garlic is minced. Add the parsley and lemon juice and pulse until the parsley is finely chopped. With the machine running, pour the ½ cup olive oil through the feed tube and process until the sauce is well blended. Set aside.

Oil the grill grate. Place the steaks directly over the hot fire. Grill the steaks on one side until nicely seared, about 2 minutes for rare and 3 minutes for medium-rare. Turn and cook until seared, 2 to 3 minutes more. Skirt steaks are too thin to yield an accurate reading with an instant-read thermometer. Instead, cut into the steak at its thickest part to check for doneness.

Transfer the steaks to a carving board and let rest for 5 minutes. Cut the meat across the grain into ¼-inch-thick slices. Arrange overlapping slices of steak on warmed dinner plates or a platter, and spoon any accumulated juices over the top. Spoon about half of the *chimichurri* over the meat, and place the rest in a bowl for passing. Serve immediately.

Skirt Steak and Grilled Fingerling Potatoes with Crumbled Blue Cheese Sauce

Here's a classic combo: grilled steak, creamy grill-roasted potatoes, and a terrific blue cheese sauce. A crisp salad, or celery and carrot sticks for dipping in the sauce, will make this a perfect weeknight meal. For the blue cheese sauce, buy a tangy, rich blue, such as Point Reyes Blue from California or Maytag Blue from Iowa.

It's easy to juggle the cooking of the potatoes and the skirt steak. I arrange the potatoes on the cool side of the grill about 10 minutes after I fire it up, so that they get a jump start on the cooking time. Since the potatoes need to be grilled with the cover on, I let them cook until they are almost done, about 18 minutes. Then I leave them on the grill, moving some to the outside edge, while I sear the steaks. This way the potatoes stay hot. See my comments in the headnote on the facing page about the preparation of skirt steak and searing it over high heat.

[SERVES 4]

2 TO 2½ POUNDS SKIRT STEAK, TRIMMED OF EXCESS FAT

2 TABLESPOONS EXTRA-VIRGIN OLIVE OIL

2 LARGE CLOVES GARLIC, MINCED

KOSHER OR SEA SALT

FRESHLY GROUND PEPPER

GRILLED FINGERLING POTATOES WITH CRUMBLED BLUE CHEESE SAUCE (PAGE 181)

Prepare a hot fire in a charcoal grill or preheat a gas grill on high. Ten minutes after the coals are lit, bank the coals to one side or turn one of the burners to low to create a cool zone.

Remove the steaks from the refrigerator 20 to 30 minutes before grilling and place them on a large, rimmed baking sheet. In a small bowl, combine the olive oil and garlic. Rub the steaks on both sides with the mixture. Lightly season the steaks on both sides with salt and pepper. While the grill is heating, put the potatoes on to cook (see headnote) and make the blue cheese sauce.

Oil the grill grate. Place the steaks directly over the hot fire. Grill the steaks on one side until nicely seared, about 2 minutes for rare and 3 minutes for medium-rare. Turn and cook until seared, 2 to 3 minutes more. Skirt steaks are too thin to yield an accurate reading with an instant-read thermometer. Instead, cut into the steak at its thickest part to check for doneness.

Transfer the steaks to a carving board and let rest for 5 minutes. Cut the meat across the grain into ¼-inch-thick slices. Arrange overlapping slices of steak on warmed dinner plates or a platter, and spoon any accumulated juices over the top. Serve the roasted potatoes on the side, spooning about half of the blue cheese sauce over the potatoes. Place the rest of the sauce in a bowl for passing. Serve immediately.

Hanger Steaks with Chile-Rubbed Grilled Onions

Often seen on restaurant menus, hanger steaks are showing up more frequently in the meat cases of supermarkets and butcher shops. They are exceptional on the grill, so if you haven't seen them, ask your butcher to order them for you. Hanger steak, or hanging tenderloin, is a tender strip of meat located on the underside of the carcass between the last rib and the loin. It has a bold beef taste and a deliciously chewy texture, and is served sliced, rather than whole. Chipotle-rubbed grilled onions are a perfect accompaniment. Complete the menu with sliced heirloom tomatoes drizzled with a peppery extra-virgin olive oil.

[SERVES 4]

1¼ TO 1½ POUNDS HANGER STEAK, TRIMMED OF FAT
1½ TABLESPOONS SOY SAUCE
1½ TABLESPOONS BALSAMIC VINEGAR
1½ TABLESPOONS WORCESTERSHIRE SAUCE
1 TABLESPOON EXTRA-VIRGIN OLIVE OIL
1 TEASPOON COARSELY GROUND PEPPER
WALLA WALLA SWEET ONIONS (PAGE 144)

Prepare a hot fire in a charcoal grill or preheat a gas grill on high.

Remove the steaks from the refrigerator 20 to 30 minutes before grilling and place them in a baking dish just large enough to hold them. In a small bowl, stir together the soy sauce, vinegar, Worcestershire sauce, olive oil, and pepper. Pour the marinade over the steaks and turn to coat both sides. While the grill is heating, prepare the onions.

Oil the grill grate. Place the steaks directly over the hot fire. Grill the steaks on one side until nicely seared, 3 minutes for rare or 4 minutes for medium-rare. Turn and cook until seared, 3 to 4 minutes more, or until an instant-read thermometer registers 120°F for rare or 130° to 135°F for medium-rare.

Transfer the steaks to a carving board and let rest for 5 minutes. While the steaks are resting, grill the onions.

Cut the meat across the grain into ½-inch-thick slices. Arrange overlapping slices of steak on warmed dinner plates, and spoon any accumulated juices over the top. Serve the onions on the side.

Buffalo Burgers with Pepper Jack Cheese

Ground buffalo has come onto the market as a wonderfully lean alternative to ground beef. Considered America's original red meat, buffalo is as tasty as beef when used for burgers, is lower in fat than choice beef, and has less cholesterol than skinless chicken breasts. Bison (the scientific name for buffalo) are natural grazers, raised on prairie grass without growth hormones or stimulants. See Sources (page 220) for mail-order information if free-range grass-fed buffalo meat is not available in your markets.

[SERVES 4]

1½ POUNDS GROUND BUFFALO

3 TABLESPOONS PLUS 1 TEASPOON GRILL EVERY DAY SPICE RUB (PAGE 31)

2 TABLESPOONS CANOLA OIL

4 SLICES PEPPER JACK CHEESE

4 SESAME-SEED HAMBURGER BUNS, SPLIT

4 LETTUCE LEAVES

1 LARGE TOMATO, SLICED

1 WALLA WALLA OR OTHER SWEET ONION, CUT INTO PAPER-THIN SLICES

MAYONNAISE

KETCHUP

RELISH

PICKLES

Prepare a hot fire in a charcoal grill or preheat a gas grill on high.

In a large bowl, combine the ground buffalo with 2 tablespoons of the spice rub, mixing well. Divide into 4 equal portions, and shape each portion into a patty 1 inch thick. Pat each patty on both sides with a teaspoon of the spice rub. Refrigerate the patties while the grill heats.

Oil the grill grate. Brush the burgers on both sides with the canola oil. Place the burgers directly over the hot fire and sear on one side, about 4 minutes. Turn and sear on the other side until juicy and medium-rare, about 4 minutes more. About a minute before the burgers are done, place a slice of cheese on top of each burger, cover the grill, and let the cheese melt. Place the buns, cut side down, on the grill to toast during the last minute the burgers are cooking.

Serve the burgers on the toasted buns with the lettuce, tomato, onion, and mayonnaise. Pass the ketchup, relish, and pickles.

The Big Beef Burger Stuffed with Blue Cheese

A grill book, especially one geared toward weeknight meals, wouldn't be complete without burger recipes. For blue cheese lovers, nothing beats a beef burger seared on the outside, with a warm nugget of melting cheese in the center. Use a tangy, full-flavored blue cheese with lots of blue veining and a hint of salt. I've kept these burgers simple, with the addition of just lettuce, tomato, and mayonnaise, but add whatever condiments you like, including bacon strips or grilled onions.

1½	POUNDS FRESHLY GROUND CHUCK
3	TABLESPOONS GRATED YELLOW ONION
1	TABLESPOON MINCED FRESH THYME
1½	TEASPOONS FRESHLY GROUND PEPPER
4	TABLESPOONS CRUMBLED BLUE CHEESE
2	TABLESPOONS CANOLA OIL
4	SESAME-SEED HAMBURGER BUNS, SPLIT
4	LETTUCE LEAVES
1	LARGE TOMATO, SLICED
	MAYONNAISE
	PICKLES

[SERVES 4]

Prepare a hot fire in a charcoal grill or preheat a gas grill on high.

In a large bowl, combine the beef, onion, thyme, and pepper and mix thoroughly. Divide into 4 equal portions and shape each portion into a ball. Press your thumb into the top of a ball, making a depression about 1 inch deep. Spoon 1 tablespoon of the cheese into the depression, press the beef over the cheese to enclose it, and shape the ball into a patty 1 inch thick. Repeat to form 3 more patties. Refrigerate the patties while the grill heats.

Oil the grill grate. Brush the burgers on both sides with the canola oil. Place the burgers directly over the hot fire and sear on one side, 4 to 5 minutes. Turn and sear on the other side until juicy and medium-rare, about 4 minutes more. Place the buns, cut side down, on the grill to toast during the last minute the burgers are cooking.

Serve the burgers on the toasted buns with the lettuce, tomato, and mayonnaise. Pass the pickles.

Char-Grilled Lamb Burgers
with Garlic-and-Mint Yogurt Sauce

My family are all lamb lovers, so during grilling season (which is nearly year-round), lamb is frequently on the fire in the form of chops, steaks, and burgers. When I was pregnant, I discovered that lamb is much easier to digest than beef, so whenever I craved red meat, I opted for lamb. These lamb burgers come off the grill seared and juicy, packed with aromatic spices and a hint of onion. Served on a grill-toasted bun, with a big dollop of mint-infused yogurt sauce, these are a Greek-food fiend's favorite burger. I often grill extra burgers and use them and the leftover sauce for a Grilled Lamb Burger and Pita Sandwich with Garlic-and-Mint Yogurt Sauce (page 198).

[SERVES 4]

1½	POUNDS FRESHLY GROUND LAMB
¼	CUP FINELY GRATED YELLOW ONION
2	TEASPOONS GROUND CUMIN
2	TEASPOONS GROUND CORIANDER
1½	TEASPOONS FRESHLY GROUND PEPPER
1	TEASPOON KOSHER OR SEA SALT
½	TEASPOON GROUND CINNAMON

GARLIC-AND-MINT
YOGURT SAUCE

1	CUP WHOLE-MILK OR LOW-FAT PLAIN YOGURT
⅓	CUP SOUR CREAM
¼	CUP FINELY CHOPPED FRESH MINT
2	TEASPOONS FRESH LIME JUICE
1	TEASPOON MINCED GARLIC
½	TEASPOON KOSHER OR SEA SALT
¼	TEASPOON FRESHLY GROUND PEPPER

2	TABLESPOONS CANOLA OIL
4	SESAME-SEED HAMBURGER BUNS, SPLIT
4	LETTUCE LEAVES

Prepare a hot fire in a charcoal grill or preheat a gas grill on high.

In a large bowl, combine the ground lamb, onion, cumin, coriander, 1¹/₂ teaspoons pepper, 1 teaspoon salt, and cinnamon and mix thoroughly. Divide into 4 equal portions, and shape each portion into a patty 1 inch thick. Refrigerate the patties while the grill heats.

To make the sauce, in a bowl, combine the yogurt, sour cream, mint, lime juice, garlic, $1/2$ teaspoon salt, and $1/4$ teaspoon pepper. Stir to combine. Set aside until ready to serve. (Leftover sauce can be covered and refrigerated for up to 3 days.)

Oil the grill grate. Brush the burgers on both sides with the canola oil. Place the burgers directly over the hot fire and sear on one side, 4 to 5 minutes. Turn and sear on the other side until juicy and cooked through with just a touch of pink, 4 to 5 minutes more. Place the buns, cut side down, on the grill to toast during the last minute the burgers are cooking.

Serve the burgers on the toasted buns with the lettuce. Top each burger with a generous spoonful of the yogurt sauce.

Lamb Steaks with *Herbes de Provence* Spice Rub

I first discovered lamb leg steaks (*culottes*) while shopping in a farmers' market in Provence. I was staying with my family and a group of friends at a rented house near Gigondas, a tiny, picturesque wine village in the Vaucluse region. The house had a full kitchen and an outdoor eating area, so we could live the French life: biking to buy warm baguettes every morning, and shopping the farmers' market for our dinner provisions, spurred on to cook by whatever looked fresh. At the market in Vaison-la-Romaine, a friendly butcher suggested we buy lamb *culottes*, steaks cut from the upper portion of the leg with a band saw. The steaks are all meat except for a small round bone, the leg bone, near the center. They are amazing on the grill, and much simpler to cook than a butterflied leg of lamb. If you don't see lamb steaks in the meat case, ask your butcher to cut them for you. Grill two extra steaks and make Grilled Lamb and Lemon Couscous Salad with Apricots and Currants (page 194) on another night.

[SERVES 4]

4   LAMB LEG STEAKS, 1 INCH THICK
    (ABOUT 9 OUNCES EACH)
    EXTRA-VIRGIN OLIVE OIL
    KOSHER OR SEA SALT
    FRESHLY GROUND PEPPER
3   TABLESPOONS *HERBES DE PROVENCE*

Prepare a hot fire in a charcoal grill or preheat a gas grill on high.

Remove the steaks from the refrigerator 20 to 30 minutes before grilling and place them on a large, rimmed baking sheet. Rub the steaks on both sides with olive oil. Liberally season the steaks on both sides with salt and pepper. Rub each steak on both sides with about 2 teaspoons of the *herbes de Provence*, lightly pressing the herbs into the meat.

Oil the grill grate. Place the steaks directly over the hot fire. Grill the steaks on one side, 4 minutes for rare or 6 minutes for medium-rare. Turn and cook for 4 minutes more, or until an instant-read thermometer registers 120°F for rare or 130° to 135°F for medium-rare.

Remove the steaks from the grill and let rest for 5 minutes before serving.

Mustard-and-Rosemary-Crusted Lamb Steaks

Once I discovered how easy it is to cook lamb leg steaks on the grill, I tried all sorts of rubs and pastes for different flavor profiles. Here's another terrific preparation. Serve the steaks with Quick-Grilled Ratatouille (page 152) or Cherry Tomato Skewers with Fresh Basil (page 138). These steaks are so fast to prepare, you'll even have time to make one of the Treasured Sides. Israeli Couscous with Zucchini, Red Bell Pepper, and Parsley (page 171) is a good choice.

[SERVES 4]

4   LAMB LEG STEAKS, 1 INCH THICK
    (ABOUT 9 OUNCES EACH)
    KOSHER OR SEA SALT
    FRESHLY GROUND PEPPER
¼   CUP DIJON MUSTARD
4   TEASPOONS FINELY MINCED
    FRESH ROSEMARY

Prepare a hot fire in a charcoal grill or preheat a gas grill on high.

Remove the steaks from the refrigerator 20 to 30 minutes before grilling and place them on a large, rimmed baking sheet. Liberally season the steaks on both sides with salt and pepper. In a small bowl, combine the mustard and rosemary. Generously brush the steaks on both sides with the mustard mixture.

Oil the grill grate. Place the steaks directly over the hot fire. Grill the steaks on one side, 4 minutes for rare or 6 minutes for medium-rare. Turn and cook for 4 minutes more, or until an instant-read thermometer registers 120°F for rare or 130° to 135°F for medium-rare.

Remove the steaks from the grill and let rest for 5 minutes before serving.

Cumin-Rubbed Lamb Chops with Moroccan Pesto Sauce

After working all day, firing up the grill and sipping a glass of wine while I prep dinner ingredients is my idea of relaxation. For this recipe, a simple cumin spice rub flavors the lamb chops, and a whirl of the food processor produces a garlic-and-cilantro-infused sauce worthy of company. Round out the menu with Eggplant with *Herbes de Provence* (page 148) and a simple mesclun salad.

[SERVES 4]

8   LAMB LOIN CHOPS, 1¼ INCHES THICK
     (ABOUT 5 OUNCES EACH)
     EXTRA-VIRGIN OLIVE OIL
2   TEASPOONS GROUND CUMIN
1½   TEASPOONS KOSHER OR SEA SALT
1½   TEASPOONS FRESHLY GROUND PEPPER
½   CUP MOROCCAN PESTO (PAGE 34)

Prepare a hot fire in a charcoal grill or preheat a gas grill on high.

Remove the chops from the refrigerator 20 to 30 minutes before grilling and place them on a large, rimmed baking sheet. Rub the lamb chops on both sides with olive oil. In a small bowl, stir together the cumin, salt, and pepper. Generously season the chops on both sides with the cumin mixture.

Oil the grill grate. Place the chops directly over the hot fire. Grill the chops on one side, 3 minutes for rare or 4 minutes for medium-rare. Turn and cook for 3 minutes more, or until an instant-read thermometer registers 120°F for rare or 130° to 135°F for medium-rare.

Remove the chops from the grill and let rest for 5 minutes. Arrange 2 chops on each warmed dinner plate and spoon some of the sauce over the top. Place the rest of the sauce in a bowl for passing. Serve immediately.

Rosemary-and-Garlic-Crusted Lamb Chops

With a quick chop-chop-chop of a chef's knife, or the whirl of a mini-chop food processor, this marinade can be ready to infuse the loin chops while the grill heats. Lamb flavored with a big hit of garlic and an overlay of rosemary is a classic combination. Serve the chops with either Orzo Salad with Kalamata Olives, Red and Yellow Bell Peppers, and Feta (page 172) or Middle Eastern Chickpea Salad (page 180).

8	LAMB LOIN CHOPS, 1¼ INCHES THICK (ABOUT 5 OUNCES EACH)
2	TABLESPOONS MINCED GARLIC (ABOUT 6 CLOVES)
3	TABLESPOONS MINCED FRESH ROSEMARY
6	TABLESPOONS EXTRA-VIRGIN OLIVE OIL
1	TEASPOON KOSHER OR SEA SALT
1	TEASPOON FRESHLY GROUND PEPPER

[SERVES 4]

Prepare a hot fire in a charcoal grill or preheat a gas grill on high.

Remove the chops from the refrigerator 20 to 30 minutes before grilling and place them on a large, rimmed baking sheet. In a small bowl, combine the garlic, rosemary, olive oil, salt, and pepper and mix thoroughly. Rub the lamb chops on both sides with the garlic mixture.

Oil the grill grate. Place the chops directly over the hot fire. Grill the chops on one side for 3 minutes for rare or 4 minutes for medium-rare. Turn and cook for 3 minutes more, or until an instant-read thermometer registers 120°F for rare or 130° to 135°F for medium-rare.

Remove the chops from the grill and let rest for 5 minutes. Arrange 2 chops on each warmed dinner plate and spoon any accumulated juices over the top. Serve immediately.

Lemongrass-Grilled Lamb Loin Chops

Lemongrass and lamb chops aren't an obvious pairing, but when I experimented with some leftover Lemongrass Paste I found in my refrigerator one day, I was delighted with the results. The lamb chops are beautifully seared with a slight charring at the bone from the sugar in the paste. The texture and lemony scent of the lemongrass, coupled with the shallots and back-bite of red pepper flakes, give the lamb an Asian flavor profile. Accompany with Baby Bok Choy (page 147) or Asian-Style Eggplant (page 149) and steamed rice.

[SERVES 4]

8   LAMB LOIN CHOPS, 1¼ INCHES THICK
    (ABOUT 5 OUNCES EACH)
½   CUP LEMONGRASS PASTE (PAGE 36)

Prepare a medium-hot fire in a charcoal grill or preheat a gas grill on medium-high.

Remove the chops from the refrigerator 20 to 30 minutes before grilling and place them on a large, rimmed baking sheet. Rub the lamb chops on both sides with the lemongrass paste.

Oil the grill grate. Place the chops directly over the medium-hot fire. Grill the chops on one side for 3 minutes for rare or 4 minutes for medium-rare. Turn and cook for 3 to 4 minutes more, or until an instant-read thermometer registers 120°F for rare or 130° to 135°F for medium-rare.

Remove the chops from the grill and let rest for 5 minutes. Arrange 2 chops on each warmed dinner plate. Serve immediately.

PORK

PORK ON THE GRILL Pork is lean, which makes it trickier to grill than other meats. It used to be fatter—in fact, at least 30 percent fatter—until growing concerns about the harmfulness of saturated fat in the American diet resulted in Congress creating the National Pork Board. In 1985, the board set goals to slim down pigs, making them leaner and more muscled. New breeding techniques and feeding programs were developed to help producers meet the goals. Today's pork, "the other white meat," is indeed better for our health, but it is also harder to keep moist and tender. The following tips and techniques will help you grill moist, flavorful, tender pork.

FIRST, with the exception of the pork satay, ham steaks, and chorizo burgers, all the recipes in this chapter call for a covered grill and two-zone fire (see page 21), for better control and timing. The best way to grill pork, whether a tenderloin or a chop, is to sear it over a medium-hot fire to create a caramelized exterior, and then to finish it over the cool zone for a moist and juicy center.

SECOND, most of us grew up hearing warnings about how undercooked pork carried trichinosis and the only way to combat the threat was to cook the meat until it was dead-and-dry-on-arrival at 180°F. It wasn't until I read Bruce Aidells's *Complete Book of Pork* that I mastered the art of cooking deliciously tender and moist pork. He argues effectively, drawing on lots of science, that pork is safely cooked when it reaches an internal temperature of 137°F and is held at that temperature for several minutes. Since then, I have cooked pork tenderloins and chops until slightly pink, which means an internal temperature of 145°F. Once the pork is allowed to rest, the carryover heat pushes the final temperature to 150° to 155°F. The meat has a faint pink appearance at the center, a slight bit of pink to the juice, and a wonderfully seared and caramelized exterior.

THIRD, never put a cold piece of pork on the grill. Remove the meat from the refrigerator 20 to 30 minutes prior to grilling. If there is any residual moisture on it, blot it dry with paper towels before marinating or using a dry rub.

FOURTH, use the right tools for turning the meat. For tenderloins and chops, I always use tongs, never a two-pronged fork, to move or turn the meat, because a fork will pierce it, allowing the juices to run out.

FINALLY, pork needs to rest when it comes off the grill. During cooking, the heat drives the juices into the cells and into the center of the meat. If you cut the pork the moment you take it off the grill, the juices will spill out on the carving board and the meat will be less tender. If you allow the pork to rest for 5 minutes before cutting into it, the juices will redistribute themselves evenly throughout the meat, leaving it juicy and tender when sliced.

Southeast Asian Pork Satay

It takes only a minute to toss all the marinade ingredients for this fabulous pork satay into a food processor. But if you want to plan ahead, you can make the marinade up to three days in advance and keep it in a covered jar in the refrigerator. Although skewers are always fun for a family meal—a good excuse for eating with your fingers—keep this recipe in mind as an appetizer for entertaining, too.

[SERVES 4]

12 10-INCH BAMBOO SKEWERS, SOAKED IN
WATER FOR 15 MINUTES, THEN DRAINED
(SEE PAGE 25)

2 PORK TENDERLOINS, 10 TO 12 OUNCES EACH,
TRIMMED OF EXCESS FAT AND SILVER SKIN

1 STALK LEMONGRASS

6 QUARTER-SIZE SLICES PEELED
FRESH GINGER

1 SHALLOT, QUARTERED

1 TABLESPOON SUGAR

1½ TEASPOONS KOSHER OR SEA SALT

1 TEASPOON GROUND CUMIN

1 TEASPOON GROUND CORIANDER

1 TEASPOON RED PEPPER FLAKES

5 TABLESPOONS VEGETABLE OIL

Immerse the skewers before lighting the grill, so they have plenty of time to soak. Prepare a medium-hot fire in a charcoal grill or preheat a gas grill on medium-high.

Remove the tenderloins from the refrigerator 20 to 30 minutes before grilling. Cut the pork on a sharp diagonal, across the grain, into ⅛-inch-thick slices and place in a large bowl.

Cut off and discard the dried, grasslike top half of the lemongrass. Trim the base from the bulb end and remove and discard the tough outer leaves. Using only the white and light green parts, cut in half lengthwise, and then cut crosswise into ½-inch pieces.

In a food processor fitted with the metal blade, combine the lemongrass, ginger, shallot, sugar, salt, cumin, coriander, and red pepper flakes and process until finely minced. With the machine running, add the vegetable oil through the feed tube and process until a paste forms. Transfer the paste to the bowl with the pork and brush or rub the paste evenly over the meat.

Thread the pork onto the skewers, dividing it evenly and weaving each slice to pierce it 2 or 3 times. Bunch the meat a bit, so it covers about 8 inches of each skewer.

Oil the grill grate. Fold a footlong piece of aluminum foil in half lengthwise and lay it on the grill grate. Arrange the skewers so the exposed bamboo is protected from the flame by the foil and the meat is directly over the fire. Use 2 pieces of foil if necessary. Grill the skewers, turning them once, until the pork is cooked through and the edges are slightly caramelized and charred, about 3 minutes per side. Serve immediately.

Latin-Rubbed Pork Tenderloin

The combination of a dry rub and grilling over direct heat provides a quick, flavorful main course with minimal effort. Pair the grilled pork with Grilled Sweet Corn, Black Bean, and Cherry Tomato Salad (page 173) or Bourbon-and-Maple-Grilled Acorn Squash (page 145).

[SERVES 6]

2 PORK TENDERLOINS, ABOUT 1 POUND EACH, TRIMMED OF EXCESS FAT AND SILVER SKIN
EXTRA-VIRGIN OLIVE OIL
¼ CUP LATIN SPICE RUB (PAGE 32)

Prepare a medium-hot fire in a charcoal grill or preheat a gas grill on medium-high.

Remove the tenderloins from the refrigerator 20 to 30 minutes before grilling and place them on a large, rimmed baking sheet. Rub the pork on all sides with olive oil. Liberally season the tenderloins on all sides with the spice rub.

To create a cool zone, bank the coals to one side of the grill or turn off one of the burners. Oil the grill grate. Place the tenderloins directly over the medium-hot fire. Grill the pork, turning to sear on all sides, for about 8 minutes. Move the tenderloins to the cooler part of the grill, cover, and grill until the meat is slightly pink in the center, or an instant-read thermometer inserted into the thickest part of a tenderloin registers 145°F, 8 to 10 minutes longer.

Transfer the pork to a carving board and let rest for 5 minutes. Cut the pork on the diagonal, across the grain, into ½-inch-thick slices and divide among warmed dinner plates. Serve immediately.

Jerk Pork Tenderloin with Grilled Pineapple

Pork tenderloin goes tropical with tart, chile-fueled flavors from the Jerk Paste and brown sugar–grilled pineapple as an accompaniment. Keep the fruit theme going with a side dish of Lemon Couscous with Dried Cranberries and Apricots (page 170).

[SERVES 6]

2	PORK TENDERLOINS, ABOUT 1 POUND EACH, TRIMMED OF EXCESS FAT AND SILVER SKIN
½	CUP JERK PASTE (PAGE 33)
3	TABLESPOONS UNSALTED BUTTER, MELTED
1	TABLESPOON PACKED DARK BROWN SUGAR
¼	TEASPOON FRESHLY GROUND PEPPER
1	RIPE PINEAPPLE, PEELED, HALVED LENGTHWISE, AND CUT CROSSWISE INTO ½-INCH-THICK SLICES

Prepare a medium-hot fire in a charcoal grill or preheat a gas grill on medium-high.

Remove the tenderloins from the refrigerator 20 to 30 minutes before grilling and place them on a large, rimmed baking sheet. Liberally rub the pork on all sides with the spice paste.

In a small bowl, combine the butter, sugar, and pepper. Stir to dissolve the sugar. Arrange the pineapple slices in a single layer on a rimmed baking sheet, and brush both sides of each slice with the butter mixture. Set aside.

Oil the grill grate. Place the pineapple directly over the medium-hot fire. Cover and grill, turning once, until grill marks appear on both sides of the slices and the pineapple is golden and tender when pierced with a knife, about 3 minutes per side. Transfer to a plate and keep warm while you grill the pork.

To create a cool zone, bank the coals to one side of the grill or turn off one of the burners. Oil the grill grate. Place the tenderloins directly over the medium-hot fire. Grill the pork, turning to sear on all sides, for about 8 minutes. Move the tenderloins to the cooler part of the grill, cover, and grill until the meat is slightly pink in the center, or an instant-read thermometer inserted into the thickest part of a tenderloin registers 145°F, 8 to 10 minutes longer.

Transfer the pork to a cutting board and let rest for 5 minutes. Cut the pork on the diagonal, across the grain, into ¹/₂-inch-thick slices and divide among warmed dinner plates. Divide the pineapple slices among the plates. Serve immediately.

Chili-Rubbed Pork Tenderloin with Nectarine Salsa

This colorful, boldly spiced summertime salsa is a good match for the smoky flavors of grilled pork. Pick nectarines that are juicy and ripe, choosing between the tarter yellow ones, for a bit of bite, and the white nectarines for their novel color and sweeter taste.

2	PORK TENDERLOINS, ABOUT 1 POUND EACH, TRIMMED OF EXCESS FAT AND SILVER SKIN
[SERVES 6]	EXTRA-VIRGIN OLIVE OIL
¼	CUP GRILL EVERY DAY SPICE RUB (PAGE 31)
4	NECTARINES, HALVED, PITTED, AND CUT INTO ½-INCH CUBES
½	CUP DICED RED ONION
½	CUP LOOSELY PACKED CHOPPED FRESH CILANTRO
NECTARINE SALSA 1	SMALL JALAPEÑO CHILE, INCLUDING SEEDS AND RIBS, MINCED (SEE COOK'S NOTE, PAGE 33)
2	TABLESPOONS FRESH LIME JUICE
1	TABLESPOON HONEY
½	TEASPOON KOSHER OR SEA SALT
¼	TEASPOON RED PEPPER FLAKES

Prepare a medium-hot fire in a charcoal grill or preheat a gas grill on medium-high.

Remove the tenderloins from the refrigerator 20 to 30 minutes before grilling and place them on a large, rimmed baking sheet. Rub the pork on all sides with olive oil. Liberally season the tenderloins on all sides with the spice rub.

While the grill is heating, make the salsa: In a bowl, combine the nectarines, onion, cilantro, jalapeño chile, lime juice, honey, salt, and red pepper flakes. Stir to combine. Set aside until ready to serve.

To create a cool zone, bank the coals to one side of the grill or turn off one of the burners. Oil the grill grate. Place the tenderloins directly over the medium-hot fire. Grill the pork, turning to sear on all sides, for about 8 minutes. Move the tenderloins to the cooler part of the grill, cover, and grill until the meat is slightly pink in the center, or an instant-read thermometer inserted into the thickest part of a tenderloin registers 145°F, 8 to 10 minutes longer.

Transfer the pork to a cutting board and let rest for 5 minutes. Cut the pork on the diagonal, across the grain, into ½-inch-thick slices and divide among warmed dinner plates. Put a large spoonful of salsa alongside the pork. Serve immediately.

Pork Tenderloin with Apricot-Mustard Glaze

Sweet and smoky because of the caramelizing of the apricot jam, this grilled pork is divine simplicity and easy for a rushed weeknight. Plus, it makes great leftovers: thinly slice the pork and layer it on a crusty French roll with a slather of mayonnaise, some arugula or romaine, and slivers of red onion. Keep a close eye on the pork while it grills. The sugar in the glaze creates a beautiful caramelized crust, but it can also char, so turning the meat so that it sears but does not burn is critical.

[SERVES 6]

2	PORK TENDERLOINS, ABOUT 1 POUND EACH, TRIMMED OF EXCESS FAT AND SILVER SKIN
¼	CUP PLUS 1 TABLESPOON DIJON MUSTARD
¼	CUP APRICOT JAM, WARMED
2	TABLESPOONS EXTRA-VIRGIN OLIVE OIL
2	LARGE CLOVES GARLIC, MINCED
2	TEASPOONS FRESHLY GROUND PEPPER

Prepare a medium-hot fire in a charcoal grill or preheat a gas grill on medium-high.

Remove the tenderloins from the refrigerator 20 to 30 minutes before grilling and place them on a large, rimmed baking sheet. In a small bowl, whisk together the mustard, jam, olive oil, garlic, and pepper until smooth to make the glaze. Set aside half the glaze and brush the pork on all sides with the rest.

To create a cool zone, bank the coals to one side of the grill or turn off one of the burners. Oil the grill grate. Place the tenderloins directly over the medium-hot fire. Grill the pork, turning to sear on all sides, for about 6 minutes. Move the tenderloins to the cooler part of the grill and brush liberally with half of the reserved glaze. Cover and grill until the meat is slightly pink in the center, or an instant-read thermometer registers 145°F when inserted into the tenderloins' thickest part, 10 to 12 minutes longer. Brush with the reserved glaze about 2 minutes before the pork is done.

Transfer the pork to a carving board and let rest for 5 minutes. Cut the pork on the diagonal, across the grain, into ½-inch-thick slices and divide among warmed dinner plates. Serve immediately.

Latin-Rubbed Pork Loin Chops with *Chimichurri*

These are pork chops with big flavor: rubbed with a heady spice mixture that mixes cumin, ginger, brown sugar, and cayenne, and then served with a garlicky lemon-infused herb sauce. Plan on a simple side dish, such as Sliced and Grilled Yukon Gold Potatoes (page 155), and a green salad or steamed vegetable.

[SERVES 4]

4 BONE-IN, CENTER-CUT PORK LOIN CHOPS,
¾ TO 1 INCH THICK (10 TO 12 OUNCES EACH)
EXTRA-VIRGIN OLIVE OIL
¼ CUP LATIN SPICE RUB (PAGE 32)
1 CUP *CHIMICHURRI* (PAGE 48)

Prepare a medium-hot fire in a charcoal grill or preheat a gas grill on medium-high.

Remove the pork chops from the refrigerator 20 to 30 minutes before grilling and place them on a rimmed baking sheet. Rub the chops on both sides with olive oil. Liberally season the chops on both sides with the spice rub. While the grill is heating, make the sauce.

To create a cool zone, bank the coals to one side of the grill or turn off one of the burners. Oil the grill grate. Place the pork chops directly over the medium-hot fire. Grill on one side until nicely seared, about 4 minutes. Turn and cook until seared, 3 to 4 minutes longer. Move the chops to the cooler part of the grill, cover, and grill until the meat is slightly pink in the center, or an instant-read thermometer registers 145°F, 10 to 12 minutes longer.

Remove the chops from the grill and let rest for 5 minutes. Transfer the chops to warmed dinner plates and spoon some of the sauce over the top. Place the rest of the sauce in a bowl for passing. Serve immediately.

Char-Grilled Pork Chops with Red Miso Barbecue Paste

Asian accents work magic on grilled pork. The combination of red miso, sesame oil, garlic, ginger, and a touch of fiery *sambal oelek* gives the pork a sweet, smoky, pungent flavor. Accompany the pork chops with rice and serve them on a bed of sautéed spinach, or with grilled Baby Bok Choy (page 147), or pair them with Asian Noodle Salad with Cilantro and Black Sesame Seeds (page 175).

[SERVES 4]

4	BONE-IN, CENTER-CUT PORK LOIN CHOPS, ¾ TO 1 INCH THICK (10 TO 12 OUNCES EACH)
½	CUP RED MISO (SEE COOK'S NOTE, FACING PAGE)
2	TABLESPOONS ASIAN SESAME OIL
2	TEASPOONS MINCED GARLIC
2	TEASPOONS PEELED AND MINCED FRESH GINGER
½	TEASPOON *SAMBAL OELEK* (SEE COOK'S NOTE, FACING PAGE)

Prepare a medium-hot fire in a charcoal grill or preheat a gas grill on medium-high.

Remove the pork chops from the refrigerator 20 to 30 minutes before grilling and place them on a rimmed baking sheet. In a small bowl, combine the miso, sesame oil, garlic, ginger, and *sambal oelek* and stir until creamy. Brush the chops on both sides with the paste.

To create a cool zone, bank the coals to one side of the grill or turn off one of the burners. Oil the grill grate. Place the pork chops directly over the medium-hot fire. Grill the pork on one side until nicely seared, about 4 minutes. Turn and cook until seared, 3 to 4 minutes longer. Move the chops to the cooler part of the grill, cover, and grill until the meat is slightly pink in the center, or an instant-read thermometer registers 145°F, 10 to 12 minutes longer.

Remove the chops from the grill and let rest for 5 minutes before serving.

COOK'S NOTE Miso, Japanese fermented soybean paste, has the consistency of creamy peanut butter and comes in a wide variety of flavors and colors. White miso, the most common type, is relatively mild and is typically blended into soups and delicate sauces. Also known as Sendai miso (for a city in northeast Honshu, Japan's largest island), the red miso used in this recipe is more fragrant and is generally used in heavier dishes. Look for miso in Japanese markets, natural-foods stores, and well-stocked supermarkets. Once opened, store it in an airtight container in the refrigerator. It will keep indefinitely.

Sambal oelek (or *sambal ulek*) is an Indonesian hot chile paste made from chiles, salt, vinegar, and sometimes garlic and tamarind. It is a fiery paste with bright flavors, and a little goes a long way. Other Asian chile pastes with garlic can be substituted, but this one is a favorite of mine. It is sold in jars in Asian markets and some supermarkets. Store it in the refrigerator once it is opened; it will keep indefinitely.

Cumin-Rubbed Pork and a Bulgur Salad
with Smoky Grilled Tomatoes and Green Onions

An easy spice rub for the pork gives you time to prepare the bulgur salad, with its melding of dynamic flavors and confetti of color from tomatoes, green onions, and parsley. Juggling the cooking of this meal is simple. Once the grill is lit, soak the bulgur, prepare the pork, then chop and measure the rest of the ingredients for the salad. There will be plenty of room on the grill to cook the pork chops and tomatoes at the same time. The chops can rest for a few minutes while you toss everything together to finish the salad. The bulgur salad calls for three Roma tomatoes; grill four extra tomatoes and serve them along with the pork and salad.

[SERVES 4]

4   BONE-IN, CENTER-CUT PORK LOIN CHOPS,
    ¾ TO 1 INCH THICK (10 TO 12 OUNCES EACH)
1   TABLESPOON GROUND CORIANDER
1   TABLESPOON GROUND CUMIN
1½ TEASPOONS KOSHER OR SEA SALT
1½ TEASPOONS FRESHLY GROUND PEPPER
2   TABLESPOONS EXTRA-VIRGIN OLIVE OIL
BULGUR SALAD WITH SMOKY GRILLED TOMATOES
AND GREEN ONIONS (PAGE 174)

Prepare a medium-hot fire in a charcoal grill or preheat a gas grill on medium-high.

Remove the pork chops from the refrigerator 20 to 30 minutes before grilling and place them on a rimmed baking sheet. In a small bowl, stir together the coriander, cumin, salt, pepper, and olive oil. Rub the chops on both sides with the spice paste. While the grill is heating, soak the bulgur for the salad, prepare the tomatoes for grilling, and chop and measure the ingredients for the salad.

To create a cool zone, bank the coals to one side of the grill or turn off one of the burners. Oil the grill grate. Place the pork chops directly over the medium-hot fire. Grill the pork on one side until nicely seared, about 4 minutes. Turn and cook until seared, 3 to 4 minutes longer. Move the chops to the cooler part of the grill, cover, and grill until the meat is slightly pink in the center, or an instant-read thermometer registers 145°F, 10 to 12 minutes longer. While the pork is cooking, make the salad.

Remove the chops from the grill and let rest for 5 minutes. Transfer the chops to warmed dinner plates and accompany with the bulgur salad. Serve immediately.

Hoisin-Basted Grilled Pork Chops

Grilled pork takes on sweet, smoky flavors when basted with an Asian-accented sauce packed with ginger, garlic, and a back bite from red pepper flakes. The chops are basted rather than marinated, so they don't char on the grill from the sugar in the sauce, and they turn out tender and moist, because they are basted frequently and finished over indirect heat. Serve the pork chops with grilled Asian-Style Eggplant (page 149) or Asparagus Spears (page 140) and Asian Noodle Salad with Cilantro and Black Sesame Seeds (page 175).

[SERVES 4]

4 BONE-IN, CENTER-CUT PORK LOIN CHOPS,
¾ TO 1 INCH THICK (10 TO 12 OUNCES EACH)
EXTRA-VIRGIN OLIVE OIL
KOSHER OR SEA SALT
FRESHLY GROUND PEPPER
1¼ CUPS HOISIN-GINGER BASTING SAUCE (PAGE 37)

Prepare a medium-hot fire in a charcoal grill or preheat a gas grill on medium-high.

Remove the pork chops from the refrigerator 20 to 30 minutes before grilling and place them on a rimmed baking sheet. Rub the pork on both sides with olive oil. Season generously on both sides with salt and pepper. Have the basting sauce in a bowl with a brush next to the grill.

To create a cool zone, bank the coals to one side of the grill or turn off one of the burners. Oil the grill grate. Place the pork chops directly over the medium-hot fire. Grill the pork on one side until nicely seared, about 4 minutes. Turn, baste with some of the sauce, and cook until seared, 3 to 4 minutes longer. Move the chops to the cooler part of the grill, baste with more sauce, cover, and grill, basting a couple more times with the remaining sauce, until the meat is slightly pink in the center, or an instant-read thermometer registers 145°F, 10 to 12 minutes longer.

Remove the chops from the grill and let rest for 5 minutes before serving.

Espresso-Cardamom-Rubbed Pork Chops with Bourbon-and-Maple-Grilled Acorn Squash

I usually make this dish in late summer or early fall when bushel baskets of winter squashes start to appear at the farmers' market. The assertive flavors of the espresso-cardamom mixture that seasons the pork are a nice counterpoint to sweet, tender squash. And, of course, it's hard to beat anything that has been basted with bourbon butter. Start the squash on the cool side of the grill about 10 minutes before you begin to grill the pork. That way, the squash and pork will be ready at about the same time. Add a romaine salad, with paper-thin slices of tart apple and a creamy vinaigrette, and your menu is complete.

[SERVES 4]

4   BONE-IN, CENTER-CUT PORK LOIN CHOPS,
    ¾ TO 1 INCH THICK (10 TO 12 OUNCES EACH)
EXTRA-VIRGIN OLIVE OIL
¼   CUP ESPRESSO-CARDAMOM RUB (PAGE 32)
BOURBON-AND-MAPLE-GRILLED ACORN SQUASH (PAGE 145)

Prepare a medium-hot fire in a charcoal grill or preheat a gas grill on medium-high.

Remove the pork chops from the refrigerator 20 to 30 minutes before grilling and place them on a rimmed baking sheet. Rub the pork on both sides with the olive oil; then with the spice rub. While the grill is heating, prepare the acorn squash for grilling, and make the bourbon-butter sauce.

To create a cool zone, bank the coals to one side of the grill or turn off one of the burners. Oil the grill grate. Place the squash on the cool side of the grill and grill according to the directions on page 145. Place the pork chops directly over the medium-hot fire. Grill the chops on one side until nicely seared, about 4 minutes. Turn and cook until seared, 3 to 4 minutes longer. Move the chops to the cooler part of the grill, cover, and grill until the pork is slightly pink in the center, or an instant-read thermometer registers 145°F, 10 to 12 minutes longer.

Remove the chops from the grill and let rest for 5 minutes. Transfer the chops to warmed dinner plates and accompany with the acorn squash. Serve immediately.

Ham Steaks with Pineapple-Jalapeño Salsa

This colorful, fiery salsa is a great partner for grilled ham steaks. Their smoky flavors and crisp, slightly charred edges complement the salsa's tropical notes. Serve slices of avocado on the side to cool the palate and balance the saltiness of the ham steaks. One jalapeño chile with the seeds and ribs made the salsa plenty hot for me, but add more if you like.

[SERVES 4]

4	BONE-IN HAM STEAKS, ABOUT ¼ INCH THICK (ABOUT 12 OUNCES EACH)
2	TABLESPOONS EXTRA-VIRGIN OLIVE OIL
	FRESHLY GROUND PEPPER

PINEAPPLE-JALAPEÑO SALSA

½	PINEAPPLE, PEELED, HALVED LENGTHWISE, CORED, AND CUT INTO ¼-INCH DICE
1	SMALL RED BELL PEPPER, SEEDED, DERIBBED, AND CUT INTO ¼-INCH DICE
2	GREEN ONIONS, INCLUDING GREEN TOPS, HALVED LENGTHWISE AND THINLY SLICED
1	JALAPEÑO CHILE, INCLUDING SEEDS AND RIBS, FINELY MINCED (SEE COOK'S NOTE, PAGE 33)
2	TABLESPOONS FRESH LIME JUICE
1	TABLESPOON PACKED LIGHT BROWN SUGAR
1	TEASPOON CHOPPED FRESH THYME
½	TEASPOON KOSHER OR SEA SALT

Prepare a medium-hot fire in a charcoal grill or preheat a gas grill on medium-high.

Remove the ham steaks from the refrigerator 20 to 30 minutes before grilling and place them on a large, rimmed baking sheet. Blot the steaks with paper towels if they are moist. Brush the steaks on both sides with olive oil and lightly season on both sides with pepper.

While the grill is heating, make the salsa: In a bowl, combine the pineapple, bell pepper, green onions, jalapeño, lime juice, sugar, thyme, and salt and mix thoroughly. Set aside.

Oil the grill grate. Place the ham steaks directly over the medium-hot fire. Grill the steaks on one side until nicely seared, 2 to 3 minutes. Turn and sear on the other side, 2 to 3 minutes longer.

Transfer the ham steaks to warmed dinner plates. Put a large spoonful of salsa on each plate. Serve immediately.

Fast-off-the-Grill Chorizo Quesadillas

Fire up the grill and toast up some of these spicy, cheesy, crispy filled tortillas. They're a snap to put together and grill, making them ideal for a casual family meal. If you decide to serve them for a party, know that they can be assembled up to an hour in advance. Grill and slice the sausages, fill the tortillas, and have them covered on a tray, ready to grill. Place them on the grill when your guests arrive, so they are gooey and hot when served.

12	OUNCES FRESH CHORIZO SAUSAGES
1	CAN (16 OUNCES) REFRIED BLACK BEANS
8	8-INCH FLOUR TORTILLAS
1½	CUPS (6 OUNCES) GRATED MONTEREY JACK CHEESE
1	CUP LOOSELY PACKED FRESH CILANTRO LEAVES
1¼	CUPS STORE-BOUGHT TOMATILLO SALSA (SEE COOK'S NOTE)
½	CUP SOUR CREAM

[SERVES 4]

Prepare a medium-hot fire in a charcoal grill or preheat a gas grill on medium-high.

Remove the sausages from the refrigerator 20 to 30 minutes before grilling.

Oil the grill grate. Place the sausages directly over the medium-hot fire. Grill the sausages, turning several times, until seared on all sides and fully cooked, 6 to 8 minutes total. Transfer the sausages to a cutting board and cut on the diagonal into ¼-inch-thick slices.

Spread 2 rounded tablespoons of the refried beans evenly over one-half of each tortilla, leaving a ½-inch border at the edges. Scatter the chorizo slices evenly over the beans. Scatter the cheese and cilantro over the sausages. Fold the tortillas over to form half-circles.

Oil the grill grate again. Using a wide spatula, carefully transfer the quesadillas to the grill. Grill on one side for about 1 minute, slide and turn the quesadillas 90 degrees, and grill until nice crosshatch grill marks appear, about 1 minute longer. Slide the spatula underneath the quesadillas and flip them. Grill until the tortillas are toasted and the cheese begins to melt, 1 to 2 minutes longer.

Transfer the quesadillas to a cutting board and cut into wedges. Serve hot with the tomatillo salsa and sour cream.

COOK'S NOTE There are plenty of tasty tomatillo salsas on the market, some sold fresh and others bottled. My favorite is a medium-hot bottled tomatillo salsa made by Frontera, created by Rick Bayless of Chicago's Frontera Grill.

Chorizo Burgers with Monterey Jack Cheese and Grilled Red Onions

For spicy burger fans, these burgers are hard to beat. Using a ratio of one part chorizo to two parts beef gives these burgers the right amount of zing and juiciness, while creating a texture that holds together. I add green onions and cilantro to the meat mixture to kick up the flavor and for a bit of color. I like to top the burgers with Monterey Jack cheese on the grill and then dress them up with grilled red onions, lettuce, and mayonnaise at the table.

	1	POUND FRESHLY GROUND CHUCK
	8	OUNCES FRESH BULK CHORIZO SAUSAGE
	2	GREEN ONIONS, INCLUDING 2 INCHES OF GREEN TOPS, VERY THINLY SLICED
	¼	CUP LOOSELY PACKED CHOPPED FRESH CILANTRO
	1	LARGE EGG, BEATEN
[SERVES 4]	1	TEASPOON KOSHER OR SEA SALT
	1	RED ONION, CUT INTO ½-INCH-THICK SLICES
	¼	CUP OLIVE OIL
	4	SLICES MONTEREY JACK CHEESE
	4	SESAME-SEED HAMBURGER BUNS, SPLIT
	4	LETTUCE LEAVES
		MAYONNAISE

Prepare a hot fire in a charcoal grill or preheat a gas grill on high.

In a large bowl, combine the ground chuck, sausage, green onions, cilantro, egg, and salt and mix thoroughly. Divide into 4 equal portions, and shape each portion into a patty 1 inch thick. Refrigerate the patties while the grill heats. Arrange the onion slices in a single layer on a rimmed baking sheet and brush on both sides with 2 tablespoons of the olive oil.

Oil the grill grate. Place the onion slices directly over the hot fire and grill, turning once, until grill marks appear on both sides and the onions are crisp-tender when pierced with a knife, about 4 minutes per side. (If you have room, grill the burgers at the same time.)

Brush the burgers on both sides with the remaining 2 tablespoons olive oil. Place the burgers directly over the hot fire and sear on one side, 3 to 4 minutes. Turn and sear on the other side until juicy and cooked through, about 4 minutes longer. Place a slice of cheese on each burger, cover the grill, and cook until the cheese is melted, about 1 minute longer. Place the buns, cut side down, on the grill to toast during the last minute while the burgers are grilling.

Serve the burgers on the toasted buns with the grilled onion slices, lettuce, and mayonnaise.

Italian Sausage Hoagies with Onions and Peppers

Sandwich nights are always a fun way to enjoy a family meal. These sausage hoagies, piled high with smoky, slightly charred peppers and onions, are served on a grill-toasted bun brushed with garlic-oregano oil. A garnish of thinly sliced *pepperoncini* adds a bit of Italian spice. Here's a thought for a great leftover: Grill two extra sausages, plus an extra onion and pepper; save them for another night, and slice and toss them with penne pasta, olive oil, cherry tomatoes, and fresh basil.

¼	CUP EXTRA-VIRGIN OLIVE OIL, PLUS MORE FOR BRUSHING
1	LARGE CLOVE GARLIC, MINCED
2	TEASPOONS DRIED OREGANO, CRUSHED
4	LARGE SWEET OR HOT FRESH ITALIAN SAUSAGES, SLIT LENGTHWISE WITHOUT CUTTING IN HALF
1	LARGE WALLA WALLA OR OTHER SWEET ONION, CUT INTO ½-INCH-THICK SLICES
1	LARGE RED BELL PEPPER, QUARTERED LENGTHWISE, SEEDED, AND DERIBBED
4	(8-INCH-LONG) CRUSTY ITALIAN SUBMARINE SANDWICH ROLLS, SPLIT
4 TO 6	LARGE *PEPPERONCINI*, CORED, SEEDED, AND THINLY SLICED

[SERVES 4]

Prepare a medium-hot fire in a charcoal grill or preheat a gas grill on medium-high.

In a small bowl, stir together the ¼ cup olive oil, the garlic, and oregano. Set aside.

Arrange the sausages on a plate and brush on all sides with olive oil. Arrange the onion slices and bell pepper pieces in a single layer on a large, rimmed baking sheet and brush on both sides with olive oil.

Oil the grill grate. Place the onion and bell pepper directly over the medium-hot fire and grill, turning once, until dark brown grill marks appear on both sides and the vegetables are crisp-tender when pierced with a knife, about 3 minutes per side. If you have room, without crowding, grill the sausages at the same time. Place the sausages, skin side down, directly over the medium-hot fire. Grill the sausages, turning once, until grill marks are etched across the sausages on both sides and they are fully cooked through, 6 to 8 minutes total. Place the rolls, cut side down, on the grill to toast during the last 30 to 60 seconds the sausages are grilling.

Transfer the grilled vegetables to a cutting board. Cut the onion slices in half and the pepper quarters lengthwise into narrow strips. Brush the toasted sides of each roll with some of the garlic oil. Place a grilled sausage on each roll bottom. Scatter the onion and pepper pieces and the *pepperoncini* over the sausages. Put the roll tops in place and serve immediately.

SEAFOOD

SEAFOOD ON THE GRILL   Mastering seafood on the grill can be a challenge, and even the most experienced grill cooks don't always succeed. While developing the recipes for my cookbook *Salmon*, there were days when I thought I was going to grow gills because I was cooking and eating so much fish. But all that trial and error resulted in my mastering techniques that are good not only for salmon, but for all seafood on the grill. Here are some simple strategies for perfectly grilled seafood.

FIRST, choose fish and shellfish that work well on the grill. For example, the recipes in this chapter call for salmon, swordfish, tuna, halibut, shrimp, and scallops. Salmon has a high oil content (and lots of good omega-3 fatty acids), which helps keep it moist on the grill. Tuna and swordfish have a dense, meaty texture that prevents them from breaking apart. Halibut and scallops are trickier, but with the right technique, they also do well on a grill. Shrimp are a cinch whether they are in their protective shell or not. All fish fillets should be at least an inch thick so they don't fall through the grill grate.

SECOND, match your seafood with the right grill method. As you'll see in the recipes, I use planks, cedar sheets, skewers, and even a bed of fresh herbs to help keep fish from sticking to the grate. Cedar or alder planks also infuse fish with a subtle wood-smoked flavor that is divine. The same is true for cedar sheets, plus opening a slightly charred, paper-thin wooden sheet to reveal a fish fillet is spectacular. Skewers allow small chunks of fish or whole shellfish to be maneuvered easily, while grilling fish on a bed of sturdy herbs, such as rosemary or thyme, imparts a lovely aroma.

THIRD, start with a clean, hot, well-oiled grill surface. Even small bits of charred food left on the grill grate will stick to a raw fish fillet and tear the flesh when you try to move it. Have the grill preheated, brush the grate so it's clean, and oil the grate thoroughly.

FOURTH, even if the fish has been seasoned with an oil-based marinade, paste, or rub, brush it or spray it on all sides with oil before putting it on the grill. This step is critical to successful fish grilling. Don't be afraid to give the fillets a good coating. It won't make the fish oily, and it will prevent it from sticking.

FINALLY, use a wide spatula or a fish spatula to turn fillets, and use tongs to turn skewers. Fish fillets need to be supported when they are turned, so having the correct tool is important. Also, turn fillets only once. The less you move them, the less likely they are to fall apart. The timings in the recipes are guidelines only, as every grill (and every fire) is slightly different. Lift the edge of a fillet to see if the flesh is nicely seared with beautiful grill marks, and then turn the fillet if it is. Use an instant-read thermometer to check for doneness.

Alder-Planked Salmon with Lemon-Vodka-Dill Marinade

I was getting ready to grill salmon one night, planning to plank the fish and use the Grill Every Day Spice Rub (page 31) on it, when I was inspired by my husband, Greg, who was making us vodka martinis with a twist of lemon. I thought, why not make a lemon-vodka marinade for the salmon? I had dill in the garden, the lemons and vodka were on the counter, and all I needed was some olive oil and seasonings. My suggestion is to make this recipe and mix a martini to go with it! Use any leftover salmon for Composed Salad of Alder-Planked Salmon and Asparagus with Lemon Vinaigrette (page 189).

1	UNTREATED ALDER PLANK, ABOUT 15 BY 7 BY ⅜ INCHES	
	(SEE COOK'S NOTE, PAGE 87)	
¼	CUP EXTRA-VIRGIN OLIVE OIL	
2	TABLESPOONS VODKA	
	FRESHLY GRATED ZEST OF 1 LEMON	
2	TABLESPOONS FRESH LEMON JUICE	
2	TABLESPOONS CHOPPED FRESH DILL	
½	TEASPOON KOSHER OR SEA SALT	
½	TEASPOON FRESHLY GROUND PEPPER	
1	WHOLE SIDE OF SALMON (ABOUT 3 POUNDS),	
	SKIN ON AND SCALED, PIN BONES REMOVED	

[SERVES 6 TO 8]

Rinse the alder plank and place it in a pan, sink, or large leakproof plastic bag filled with water. Soak the plank for at least 20 minutes. (The plank can be submerged in water and left to soak all day, so plan ahead and soak the plank before you leave for work.)

Prepare a medium fire in a charcoal grill or preheat a gas grill on medium.

In a small bowl, combine the olive oil, vodka, lemon zest, lemon juice, dill, salt, and pepper and mix thoroughly. Place the whole salmon fillet on a large, rimmed baking sheet and pour the marinade evenly over the top. Set aside while the grill heats.

When ready to grill, place the soaked plank on the grill grate directly over the medium fire and cover. After a few minutes, the plank will begin to smoke and crackle. Turn the plank over, re-cover, and "toast" the other side for about 2 minutes. Uncover the grill, transfer the salmon fillet to the plank, and then re-cover the grill. Cook the salmon until it is almost opaque throughout but still very moist when tested with a knife, or an instant-read thermometer inserted in the center registers 125° to 130°F, 15 to 25 minutes, >>

Alder-Planked Salmon with Lemon-Vodka-Dill Marinade
(continued)

depending on the thickness of the fillet. (Keep a spray bottle with water nearby in case the plank gets too hot and begins to flame. Extinguish the flame and continue grilling the salmon, adjusting the heat level if necessary.)

Using 2 long spatulas, transfer the salmon to a warmed platter. Use tongs, heatproof gloves, or the spatulas to remove the plank from the heat and set it aside to cool. Cut the salmon into individual servings and serve immediately. Alternatively, for a rustic presentation, leave the salmon on the plank and place the plank on a large heatproof platter.

Alder-Planked Salmon with Fresh Herbs

For hundreds of years, Native Americans living in the Pacific Northwest have cooked fish— salmon in particular—by planking it. They build a huge fire pit, attach sides of salmon to planks, and then drive the bottom of the planks into the ground so the salmon slowly grill-roasts vertically next to the fire. The technique I describe here is much simpler!

Grilling salmon on a wood plank imparts a sweet, smoky, slightly charred flavor to the fish. The possibilities for flavor depend on the type of wood you use—alder, cedar, or oak— and the sauce, marinade, or rub you choose. This recipe explains the basics of grilling fish on a plank and gives a delicious flavor combination: herb-rubbed salmon on an alder plank. An alternative would be to rub the salmon fillet with olive oil and a few tablespoons of the Grill Every Day Spice Rub (page 31).

1	UNTREATED ALDER PLANK, ABOUT 15 BY 7 BY ³⁄₈ INCHES (SEE COOK'S NOTE)
1	WHOLE SIDE OF SALMON (ABOUT 3 POUNDS), SKIN ON AND SCALED, PIN BONES REMOVED
	EXTRA-VIRGIN OLIVE OIL
	KOSHER OR SEA SALT
	FRESHLY GROUND PEPPER
	LEAVES FROM 4 SPRIGS FRESH THYME
	LEAVES FROM 4 SPRIGS FRESH ROSEMARY
½	LEMON

[SERVES 6 TO 8]

Rinse the alder plank and place it in a pan, sink, or large leakproof plastic bag filled with water. Soak the plank for at least 20 minutes. (The plank can be submerged in water and left to soak all day, so plan ahead and soak the plank before you leave for work.)

Prepare a medium fire in a charcoal grill or preheat a gas grill on medium.

Rub the salmon with olive oil and sprinkle lightly on both sides with salt and pepper. Scatter the thyme and rosemary leaves over the flesh, pressing them lightly so they adhere to the flesh. Set aside while the grill heats.

When ready to grill, place the soaked plank on the grill grate directly over the medium fire and cover. After a few minutes, the plank will begin to smoke and crackle. Turn the plank over, re-cover, and "toast" the other side for about 2 minutes. Uncover the grill, transfer the whole salmon fillet to the plank, and then re-cover the grill. Cook the salmon until it is almost opaque throughout but still very moist when tested with a knife, or an instant-read thermometer inserted in the center registers 125° to 130°F, 15 to 25 minutes, depending on the thickness of the fillet. (Keep a spray bottle with water nearby in case the plank gets too hot and begins to flame. Extinguish the flame and continue grilling the salmon, adjusting the heat level if necessary.)

Using 2 long spatulas, transfer the salmon to a warmed platter. Use tongs, heatproof gloves, or the spatulas to remove the plank from the heat and set it aside to cool. Squeeze the lemon half over the salmon, cut into individual servings, and serve immediately. Alternatively, for a rustic presentation, leave the salmon on the plank and place the plank on a large heatproof platter.

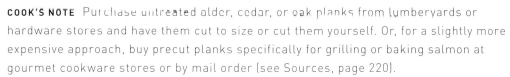

COOK'S NOTE Purchase untreated alder, cedar, or oak planks from lumberyards or hardware stores and have them cut to size or cut them yourself. Or, for a slightly more expensive approach, buy precut planks specifically for grilling or baking salmon at gourmet cookware stores or by mail order (see Sources, page 220).

A plank can be reused if it isn't too charred or cracked. Once the plank has cooled, brush it clean with a grill brush, set it upright to dry, and then store it in a brown paper bag. Resoak it before using.

Honey-Soy-Lacquered Salmon with Cilantro Noodles

Sweet and smoky grilled salmon paired with a light Asian noodle salad is carefree summer weeknight cooking at its best. No need to boil noodles or wash a pot for this dish. The bean thread noodles just need to soften in a bowl of hot water while the grill heats. The glaze and salad dressing are a snap to make, which means everything is ready in about a half hour.

[SERVES 4]

3   PACKAGES (2 OUNCES EACH) BEAN THREAD
    NOODLES (SEE COOK'S NOTE, PAGE 175)
4   CENTER-CUT SALMON FILLETS (ABOUT
    6 OUNCES EACH), SKIN ON AND SCALED,
    PIN BONES REMOVED
EXTRA-VIRGIN OLIVE OIL
KOSHER OR SEA SALT

½   TEASPOON FRESHLY GROUND PEPPER;
    PLUS MORE FOR SPRINKLING
5   TABLESPOONS SOY SAUCE
3   TABLESPOONS HONEY
3   TABLESPOONS ASIAN SESAME OIL
2   TEASPOONS FRESH LEMON JUICE
½   CUP PACKED FRESH CILANTRO
    LEAVES, COARSELY CHOPPED
2   TABLESPOONS BLACK SESAME SEEDS

Prepare a medium-hot fire in a charcoal grill or preheat a gas grill on medium-high.

In a large bowl, soak the noodles in hot water to cover until softened, about 20 minutes.

Generously brush the salmon fillets on both sides with olive oil and sprinkle lightly with salt and pepper. To make the glaze, in a small bowl, combine 1 tablespoon of the soy sauce, 2 tablespoons of the honey, and ½ teaspoon pepper and mix thoroughly. Set aside.

To make the dressing, in a small bowl, combine the remaining 4 tablespoons soy sauce and 1 tablespoon honey, the sesame oil, and the lemon juice, mixing well.

Drain the noodles well in a colander, shaking the colander a few times to make sure all the water is removed. Pat the noodles dry with paper towels. Toss the noodles with the dressing, cilantro, and sesame seeds. Set aside.

Oil the grill grate. Use tongs to arrange the salmon fillets, flesh side down, directly over the medium-hot fire. Grill the salmon until grill marks are etched across the fillets, about 3 minutes. Turn the fillets, skin side down, and brush the salmon flesh generously with the glaze. Cover the grill and continue grilling the salmon until it is almost opaque throughout but still very moist when tested with a knife, or an instant-read thermometer inserted in the center registers 125° to 130°F, 3 to 4 minutes longer.

Divide the noodles among dinner plates. Using a wide spatula, place a salmon fillet in the center of each plate, on top of the noodles. Serve immediately.

Salmon Grilled on a Bed of Herbs

In this recipe, the salmon cooks up sweet and smoky due to the aromatic herbs. This technique also takes the fear out of grilling fish, because the herbs keep the salmon from sticking to the grill. Serve with Mixed Grill of Zucchini and Yellow Summer Squash with Pesto Oil (page 143), or make the Israeli Couscous with Zucchini, Red Bell Pepper, and Parsley (page 171).

[SERVES 4]

4   CENTER-CUT SALMON FILLETS (ABOUT 6 OUNCES EACH),
     SKIN ON AND SCALED, PIN BONES REMOVED
EXTRA-VIRGIN OLIVE OIL
KOSHER OR SEA SALT
FRESHLY GROUND PEPPER
8   SPRIGS FRESH THYME
8   SPRIGS FRESH ROSEMARY
1   LEMON, CUT INTO 8 THIN SLICES

Prepare a medium fire in a charcoal grill or preheat a gas grill on medium.

Generously brush the salmon fillets on both sides with olive oil and sprinkle lightly with salt and pepper. Lay 2 thyme sprigs and 2 rosemary sprigs on the flesh side of each fillet, pressing them lightly so they adhere to the flesh.

Oil the grill grate. Use tongs to arrange the salmon fillets, herb side down, directly over the medium fire and cover. Grill the salmon until grill marks are etched across the fillets, about 3 minutes. Turn the fillets, re-cover, and cook until the salmon is almost opaque throughout but still very moist when tested with a knife, or an instant-read thermometer inserted in the center registers 125° to 130°F, 3 to 4 minutes longer.

Using tongs or a wide spatula, transfer the fillets to warmed dinner plates. Remove the herbs from the salmon, arrange 2 slices of lemon on each plate, and serve immediately.

Salmon Wrapped in Cedar Wood Sheets

A few years ago, I read about cedar sheets for cooking in the dining section of the *New York Times* and decided they would be great for grilling salmon. A box of 100 sheets cost seventy-two dollars from Korin Japanese Trading Company in New York. Even though it was a lot of sheets and they were rather costly, I ordered a box, justifying the purchase as a professional expense. I wanted to share this recipe, but I felt I couldn't because of both the quantity and the price. Then, one day while I was browsing on the Internet, I saw a Web site that sold the sheets in smaller quantities better suited for the home cook. (See the Cook's Note for details.) I'm delighted to include this recipe; it's easy for a weeknight and an eye-catching presentation for entertaining.

4	SHEETS CEDAR PAPER, EACH 6 INCHES SQUARE (SEE COOK'S NOTE, PAGE 92)
4	CENTER-CUT SALMON FILLETS (ABOUT 5 INCHES LONG AND 2 INCHES WIDE), SKIN AND PIN BONES REMOVED
	EXTRA-VIRGIN OLIVE OIL
	KOSHER OR SEA SALT
	FRESHLY GROUND PEPPER
8	SPRIGS FRESH THYME
8	SPRIGS FRESH ROSEMARY
1	LEMON, CUT INTO 8 PAPER-THIN SLICES
4	GREEN ONIONS WITH LONG GREEN TOPS

[SERVES 4]

Prepare a medium fire in a charcoal grill or preheat a gas grill on medium.

Soak the cedar paper sheets in warm water until pliable, 5 to 10 minutes.

Generously brush the salmon fillets on both sides with olive oil and sprinkle lightly with salt and pepper. Lay 2 thyme sprigs and 2 rosemary sprigs on each fillet, pressing them lightly so they adhere to the flesh. Arrange 2 lemon slices, overlapping them slightly, over the top of the herbs on each fillet.

Place the 4 sheets of soaked cedar on a work surface. Place a salmon fillet in the center of each sheet, parallel to the grain of the wood. Cut 8 long strips from the green tops of the onions to use as ties. Working with 1 cedar sheet at a time, bring up the sides to encase the piece of salmon, forming a tube and overlapping the edges if possible. Wrap a long strip of green onion around the tube about one-third of the way down from the top edge, and tie it gently to secure the tube. Wrap another strip of green onion about one-third of the way up from the bottom edge and tie it. Repeat to secure the other packets. >>

Salmon Wrapped in Cedar Wood Sheets
(continued)

Oil the grill grate. Use tongs to arrange the cedar packets, edge side up, directly over the medium fire and cover. Grill until the packets begin to smoke and crackle, about 4 minutes. Turn the packets over, re-cover the grill, and "toast" the other side until the salmon is almost opaque throughout but still very moist when tested with a knife, or an instant-read thermometer inserted in the center registers 125° to 130°F, 3 to 4 minutes longer.

Using tongs, transfer the salmon packets to warmed dinner plates. Snip the onions with a knife and use the tongs to open the packets and unroll the wood sheets. Serve immediately.

 COOK'S NOTE Cedar sheets are pliable, smooth, and paper-thin. They come in 6-inch squares, just the right size to enclose a single serving of salmon. The sheets must be soaked in water to minimize charring and to become pliable before they can be placed on the grill grate. You can use either a couple of long green onion tops or leek greens, depending on the recipe, to secure a cedar-sheet package closed. The sheets, also called cedar grilling papers, can be ordered in small quantities online from www.barbecuewood. com, or you can order them in larger quantities from www.korin.com. (See Sources, page 220.)

Lemon-and-Oregano-Grilled Halibut Skewers

Firm, meaty halibut is a terrific fish to grill because it doesn't break apart easily and it works well with different flavor profiles. For this recipe, I have marinated the halibut in a tasty oregano vinaigrette, saving a couple of tablespoons to brush on the fish when it comes off the grill. Serve the skewers with Orzo Salad with Kalamata Olives, Red and Yellow Bell Peppers, and Feta (page 172).

[SERVES 4]

4	10-INCH BAMBOO SKEWERS, SOAKED IN WATER FOR 15 MINUTES, THEN DRAINED (SEE PAGE 25)
1/3	CUP EXTRA-VIRGIN OLIVE OIL, PLUS MORE FOR BRUSHING
2	TABLESPOONS FRESH LEMON JUICE
2	TABLESPOONS FINELY MINCED SHALLOTS
2	TABLESPOONS FINELY MINCED FRESH OREGANO
3/4	TEASPOON FRESHLY GROUND PEPPER
1/2	TEASPOON KOSHER OR SEA SALT
1/8	TEASPOON GARLIC POWDER
1 1/2	POUNDS HALIBUT FILLETS, SKIN REMOVED, CUT INTO 1 1/2-INCH CHUNKS

Immerse the skewers before lighting the grill so they have plenty of time to soak. Prepare a medium-hot fire in a charcoal grill or preheat a gas grill on medium-high.

In a bowl, combine the ⅓ cup olive oil, the lemon juice, shallots, oregano, pepper, salt, and garlic powder and mix well. Reserve 2 tablespoons of the marinade. Put the halibut chunks in the marinade and toss to coat all sides. Set aside while the grill heats.

Thread the halibut onto skewers, dividing it evenly and covering about 8 inches of each skewer. Just before grilling, brush the halibut with olive oil to keep it from sticking to the grill grate.

Oil the grill grate. Fold a footlong piece of aluminum foil in half lengthwise and lay it on the grill grate. Arrange the skewers so the exposed bamboo is protected from the flame by the foil and the meat is directly over the fire. Grill the skewers, turning them as each side browns, until the fish is just opaque in the center when tested with a knife, about 5 minutes total.

Arrange the skewers on warmed dinner plates and brush with the reserved marinade. Serve immediately.

Halibut with Salsa Verde

The milky white, firm flesh of halibut stands up well on the grill, and the resulting sweet, smoky fillet, with slightly charred edges, is a perfect partner to an assertive sauce. This recipe marries the fish with a salsa verde, an herb-infused emulsion packed with the big flavors of garlic and anchovy. To keep the fillets from sticking, clean the grill grate thoroughly and slick the fillets with oil. Once on the grill, leave the fillets undisturbed until it is time to flip them. This will prevent the flesh from sticking and tearing.

[SERVES 4]

¼	CUP EXTRA-VIRGIN OLIVE OIL
2	TEASPOONS FRESHLY GRATED LEMON ZEST
½	TEASPOON KOSHER OR SEA SALT
¼	TEASPOON RED PEPPER FLAKES
4	HALIBUT FILLETS, 1 TO 1¼ INCHES THICK (ABOUT 6 OUNCES EACH), SKIN REMOVED

SALSA VERDE

1	CUP LOOSELY PACKED FRESH FLAT-LEAF PARSLEY LEAVES
2	TABLESPOONS CAPERS, RINSED AND DRAINED
2	OIL-PACKED ANCHOVY FILLETS, PATTED DRY AND MINCED
1	LARGE CLOVE GARLIC
2	TEASPOONS RED WINE VINEGAR
½	CUP EXTRA-VIRGIN OLIVE OIL

Prepare a medium-hot fire in a charcoal grill or preheat a gas grill on medium-high.

In a baking dish large enough to hold the halibut in a single layer, combine the ¼ cup olive oil, the lemon zest, salt, and red pepper flakes. Stir to blend thoroughly. Add the halibut fillets and turn to coat both sides. Set aside.

While the grill is heating, make the salsa: In a food processor fitted with the metal blade, combine the parsley, capers, anchovies, garlic, and vinegar and process until minced. With the machine running, add the ½ cup olive oil through the feed tube and process until emulsified. Transfer the salsa to a bowl and set aside.

Oil the grill grate. Use tongs to arrange the halibut fillets, flesh side down, directly over the medium-hot fire and cover. Grill the halibut until grill marks are etched across the fillets, about 3 minutes. Turn the fillets and re-cover the grill. Cook until the halibut is almost opaque throughout but still very moist when tested with a knife, or an instant-read thermometer inserted in the center registers 125° to 130°F, 2 to 3 minutes longer.

Using tongs or a wide spatula, transfer the fillets to warmed dinner plates, and accompany each fillet with a spoonful of the salsa. Serve immediately.

Halibut with Chipotle Sauce

Here, the mildness of the halibut plays off of the rich, spicy chile sauce. There is usually sauce left over, so I like to grill two or three extra fillets and make grilled halibut tacos on another night. Just wrap warm corn tortillas around grilled halibut chunks, shredded cabbage or crisp lettuce, chopped green onions and tomatoes, and a spoonful of sauce— a dynamite dinner of Baja fish tacos in record time.

[SERVES 4]

¼ CUP EXTRA-VIRGIN OLIVE OIL
½ TEASPOON KOSHER OR SEA SALT
¼ TEASPOON FRESHLY GROUND PEPPER
¼ TEASPOON RED PEPPER FLAKES
4 HALIBUT FILLETS, 1 TO 1¼ INCHES THICK (ABOUT 6 OUNCES EACH), SKIN REMOVED

CHIPOTLE SAUCE

1 CUP MAYONNAISE
3 TABLESPOONS BUTTERMILK OR SOUR CREAM
2 CANNED CHIPOTLE CHILES IN ADOBO SAUCE, MINCED
2 TABLESPOONS MINCED FRESH CILANTRO
¼ TEASPOON KOSHER OR SEA SALT

Prepare a medium-hot fire in a charcoal grill or preheat a gas grill on medium-high.

In a baking dish large enough to hold the halibut in a single layer, combine the olive oil, ½ teaspoon salt, the pepper, and red pepper flakes. Stir to blend thoroughly. Add the halibut fillets and turn to coat on both sides. Set aside.

While the grill is heating, make the sauce: In a small bowl, combine the mayonnaise, buttermilk, chiles, cilantro, and ¼ teaspoon salt and mix well. Set aside.

Oil the grill grate. Use tongs to arrange the halibut fillets, flesh side down, directly over the medium-hot fire and cover. Grill the halibut until grill marks are etched across the fillets, about 3 minutes. Turn the fillets and re-cover the grill. Cook until the halibut is almost opaque throughout but still very moist when tested with a knife, or an instant-read thermometer inserted in the center registers 125° to 130°F, 2 to 3 minutes longer.

Using tongs or a spatula, transfer the fillets to warmed dinner plates, and accompany each fillet with a spoonful of the sauce. Serve immediately.

Chile-and-Peanut-Crusted Halibut

Trader Joe's, a specialty-foods store with over 250 stores across the United States, always has an interesting selection of seasoned nuts for snacking. I bought some Thai lime and chile peanuts to serve with margaritas for a party, and decided they would be fabulous crushed and pressed into the top of halibut fillets for the grill. I consistently see these nuts in my local store, so if there is a Trader Joe's near you, I hope you will see them, as well. If not, pick differently seasoned peanuts, or even seasoned cashews or hazelnuts, and follow the technique explained in the recipe. Serve the halibut with grilled Baby Bok Choy (page 147).

[SERVES 4]

4 HALIBUT FILLETS, 1 TO 1¼ INCHES THICK
(ABOUT 6 OUNCES EACH), SKIN REMOVED
2 TO 3 TABLESPOONS EXTRA-VIRGIN OLIVE OIL
⅔ CUP THAI LIME AND CHILE PEANUTS (SEE COOK'S NOTE)
1 LIME, QUARTERED

Prepare a medium-hot fire in a charcoal grill or preheat a gas grill on medium-high.

Arrange the halibut fillets on a rimmed baking sheet and brush or rub on both sides with the olive oil. Put the peanuts in a heavy-duty lock-top plastic bag. Use a rolling pin or the bottom of a small, heavy saucepan to crush the nuts finely. Crush them just enough to create small pieces without turning them to meal. Divide the nuts into 4 equal portions, and press a portion into the top, or flesh side, of each fillet, creating a crust.

To create a cool zone, bank the coals to one side of the grill or turn off one of the burners. Oil the grill grate. Using a spatula, transfer the halibut fillets, nut-crusted side up, directly over the medium-hot fire and cover. Grill the halibut until grill marks are etched across the fillets, about 3 minutes. Use a spatula to move the fillets to the cool side of the grill. Re-cover and grill until the halibut is almost opaque throughout but still very moist when tested with a knife, or an instant-read thermometer inserted in the center registers 125° to 130°F, 4 to 5 minutes longer.

Using a spatula, transfer the fillets to warmed dinner plates, and place a lime wedge on each plate. Serve immediately.

COOK'S NOTE Thai lime and chile peanuts are available in 1-pound cellophane bags at Trader Joe's (see Sources, page 220). They have a distinct tart lime flavor and a real kick of heat from the ground chile.

Pepper-Crusted Ahi Tuna with a Black Tapenade Sauce

Grilled rare tuna steaks are sweet and mildly oceanic, with a flash of crusty grill flavor on the outside and a beefy texture on the inside. A coat of crushed peppercorns and a final flourish of black olive tapenade add just the right amount of savoriness for a first-rate weeknight meal. Plan ahead and make grilled New Potatoes Tossed with Extra-Virgin Olive Oil and *Fleur de Sel* (page 154) to serve with the tuna. Grill two extra tuna steaks and use them to prepare Pepper-Crusted Ahi Tuna Salad Niçoise (page 187) on another night.

[SERVES 4]

2 TABLESPOONS EXTRA-VIRGIN OLIVE OIL

⅓ CUP STORE-BOUGHT BLACK OLIVE TAPENADE

2 TABLESPOONS KOSHER OR SEA SALT

⅓ CUP COARSELY CRUSHED PEPPERCORNS

4 AHI TUNA STEAKS, 1¼ INCHES THICK
(ABOUT 5 OUNCES EACH)

Prepare a hot fire in a charcoal grill or preheat a gas grill on high.

In a small bowl, combine the olive oil and tapenade and mix well. Set aside.

On a dinner plate, mix together the salt and peppercorns and spread the mixture out on the plate. Press each tuna steak into the mixture, coating it heavily on both sides. Set aside on a separate plate.

Oil the grill grate. Use tongs to arrange the steaks directly over the hot fire. Grill the tuna until grill marks are etched across the steaks, about 2 minutes. Turn the steaks and grill until red-rare in the center when tested with a knife, or an instant-read thermometer inserted in the center registers 120°F, about 2 minutes longer.

Use tongs to transfer the steaks to a cutting board and cut across the grain into ¼-inch-thick slices. Arrange the slices, overlapping them, on warmed dinner plates, and accompany with a spoonful of the sauce. Serve immediately.

Tuscan Olive Oil–Basted Swordfish
with Grilled Peppers and Olives

One look at and one taste of this dish, and you know you've grilled a winner. Use a fruity extra-virgin olive oil from Tuscany, especially one with a peppery finish on the palate. Give the swordfish fillets and peppers a generous rub, so the oil penetrates them while the grill heats. Basting the fish while it grills, but being careful to avoid flare-ups, will give the grilled fish an appealing smoky flavor.

4	SWORDFISH FILLETS (6 TO 7 OUNCES EACH), SKIN REMOVED
	TUSCAN EXTRA-VIRGIN OLIVE OIL
	KOSHER OR SEA SALT
	FRESHLY GROUND PEPPER
2	RED BELL PEPPERS, SEEDED, DERIBBED, AND CUT LENGTHWISE INTO 6 STRIPS EACH
2	YELLOW BELL PEPPERS, SEEDED, DERIBBED, AND CUT LENGTHWISE INTO 6 STRIPS EACH
1	CUP PITTED SICILIAN-STYLE GREEN OLIVES, QUARTERED

[SERVES 4]

Prepare a medium-hot fire in a charcoal grill or preheat a gas grill on medium-high.

Arrange the fillets on a rimmed baking sheet and rub generously on both sides with olive oil. Sprinkle lightly on both sides with salt and pepper. Set aside. In a bowl, toss the peppers with olive oil to coat. Set aside.

Oil the grill grate. Use tongs to arrange the bell peppers directly over the medium-hot fire and cook, turning once, until light grill marks appear, about 2 minutes per side. Transfer to a warmed platter or rimmed baking sheet and keep warm.

Oil the grill grate again. Use tongs to arrange the swordfish fillets directly over the medium-hot fire and cook, basting frequently with olive oil, until grill marks are etched across the fillets, about 3 minutes. Turn the fillets and cook, continuing to baste frequently, until almost opaque throughout but still very moist when tested with a knife, or an instant-read thermometer inserted in the center registers 125° to 130°F, about 3 minutes longer.

Arrange a mixture of yellow and red peppers on each warmed dinner plate. Place a fillet on top, and scatter some olives over the fish. Serve immediately, with a drizzle of olive oil, if desired.

Chili-Rubbed Shrimp with Soft Tacos and Salsa

Here's a plan for two meals from one night of grilling: Make grilled shrimp tacos one night and a main-course salad another night. While you prep the shrimp tacos, grill an extra 12 ounces shrimp and refrigerate them. A night or two later, make the Shrimp, Pineapple, and Anaheim Chile Salad with Avocado (page 201) for a light, refreshing main course. Complete the menu with crusty artisanal bread or a bowl of crispy tortilla chips.

	1	POUND LARGE SHRIMP (26/30 COUNT), PEELED AND DEVEINED, TAILS REMOVED
	2	TABLESPOONS GRILL EVERY DAY SPICE RUB (PAGE 31)
	1	LIME, QUARTERED
	2	CUPS SHREDDED ICEBERG LETTUCE
[SERVES 4]	¾	CUP LOOSELY PACKED FRESH CILANTRO LEAVES
	1	LARGE, RIPE TOMATO, CORED, HALVED CROSSWISE, SEEDED, AND CHOPPED
	2	LARGE HASS AVOCADOS, HALVED, PITTED, PEELED, AND CUT INTO THIN WEDGES
	1 TO 1½	CUPS STORE-BOUGHT SALSA
	8	8-INCH FLOUR TORTILLAS

Prepare a medium-hot fire in a charcoal grill or preheat a gas grill on medium-high.

In a bowl, toss the shrimp with the spice rub until well coated.

Arrange the lime, lettuce, cilantro, tomato, avocados, and salsa in separate small serving bowls and have them ready for assembling the tacos.

Oil the grill grate. Arrange the shrimp directly over the medium-hot fire and grill, turning once, until the shrimp turn pink on the outside and are just opaque on the inside, about 2 minutes per side. While the shrimp are cooking, grill the tortillas. Depending on the size of the grill, lay I or 2 tortillas on the grill at a time, warming them over direct heat for about 15 seconds per side. Stack them on a plate and keep warm. Transfer the shrimp to a serving bowl.

Let diners assemble their own tacos. To assemble, place 2 or 3 shrimp in a tortilla, squeeze a bit of lime juice over the shrimp, and mound lettuce, cilantro, tomato, and avocado on top. Finally, add a spoonful of salsa. Serve with plenty of napkins!

Shrimp and Pineapple Skewers
with Garlic and Cilantro Drizzle

These colorful, easy-to-prepare shrimp skewers make a delightful main course. The garlic and cilantro drizzle slicks the shrimp and pineapple, making every bite a fusion of flavor. Accompany the skewers with rice or with Lemon Couscous with Dried Cranberries and Apricots (page 170). The skewers would also be a great appetizer for a big backyard party; just double or triple the recipe to serve a crowd.

[SERVES 4]

8   (10-INCH) BAMBOO SKEWERS, SOAKED IN WATER
    FOR 15 MINUTES, THEN DRAINED (SEE PAGE 25)
1   POUND LARGE SHRIMP (26/30 COUNT), PEELED
    AND DEVEINED, TAILS REMOVED
2   RED BELL PEPPERS, SEEDED, DERIBBED, AND
    CUT INTO 1-INCH SQUARES (ABOUT 24 PIECES)
½   PINEAPPLE, PEELED, HALVED, CORED, AND
    CUT INTO 1-INCH CUBES (ABOUT 24 PIECES)

6   TABLESPOONS EXTRA-VIRGIN OLIVE OIL,
    PLUS MORE FOR BRUSHING
1½ TABLESPOONS FRESH LIME JUICE
2   CLOVES GARLIC, MINCED
1½ TABLESPOONS MINCED FRESH CILANTRO
½   TEASPOON KOSHER OR SEA SALT
½   TEASPOON SUGAR
½   TEASPOON FRESHLY GROUND PEPPER

Immerse the skewers before lighting the grill so they have plenty of time to soak. Prepare a medium-hot fire in a charcoal grill or preheat a gas grill on medium-high.

To assemble the skewers, pinch a shrimp into a horseshoe shape and thread it onto a skewer, piercing it once near the tail end and again near the head end. Follow with a square of red pepper and a cube of pineapple. Repeat the lineup three more times, then load the remaining 7 skewers the same way. Arrange the skewers on a rimmed baking sheet and brush them with olive oil. Set aside.

While the grill is heating, prepare the sauce: In a small bowl, combine the 6 tablespoons olive oil, the lime juice, garlic, cilantro, salt, sugar, and pepper. Stir to mix, and set aside.

Oil the grill grate. Fold a footlong piece of aluminum foil in half lengthwise and lay it on the grill grate. Arrange the skewers so the exposed bamboo is protected from the flame by the foil and the food is directly over the medium-hot fire. Use 2 pieces of foil if necessary. Grill on one side until light grill marks appear on the shrimp and the pineapple begins to caramelize, about 3 minutes. Turn and grill until the shrimp turn pink on the outside and are just opaque on the inside, about 3 minutes longer.

Arrange 2 skewers on each warmed dinner plate, and drizzle the garlic and cilantro sauce over the skewers. Serve immediately.

Scallop Brochettes with Green Onions and Mango Salsa

Done right, scallops on the grill are sweet and moist on the inside and etched with grill marks on the outside, picking up just enough char at the edges to accent the flavor of the sea. The marinade boasts big flavor, and the fruity-hot salsa complements the brochettes. I have included the recipe for my favorite homemade mango salsa, but if you're pressed for time, buy a good-quality mango salsa.

8	10-INCH BAMBOO SKEWERS, SOAKED IN WATER FOR 15 MINUTES, THEN DRAINED (SEE PAGE 25)
24	LARGE SEA SCALLOPS (1¼ TO 1½ POUNDS)
¼	CUP EXTRA-VIRGIN OLIVE OIL, PLUS MORE FOR BRUSHING
2	TABLESPOONS FRESH LEMON JUICE
1	LARGE CLOVE GARLIC, MINCED
1	TABLESPOON MINCED FRESH CILANTRO
¼	TEASPOON KOSHER OR SEA SALT
¼	TEASPOON FRESHLY GROUND PEPPER
2	RED BELL PEPPERS, SEEDED, DERIBBED, AND CUT INTO 1-INCH SQUARES (ABOUT 24 PIECES)
4	GREEN ONIONS, INCLUDING GREEN TOPS, CUT INTO 1-INCH LENGTHS
1 TO 1½ CUPS MANGO SALSA, HOMEMADE (PAGE 106) OR STORE-BOUGHT	

[SERVES 4]

Immerse the skewers before lighting the grill so they have plenty of time to soak. Prepare a medium-hot fire in a charcoal grill or preheat a gas grill on medium-high.

Rinse the scallops under cold water to remove any small particles of grit. Remove any tough muscle on the side of each scallop. Pat the scallops dry with paper towels.

While the grill is heating, prepare the sauce: In a small bowl, combine the ¼ cup olive oil, the lemon juice, garlic, cilantro, salt, and pepper. Stir to mix thoroughly. Set aside until ready to serve.

To assemble the skewers, thread a scallop through its side onto a skewer. Follow with a square of red pepper and piece of green onion. Repeat the lineup three more times, then load the remaining 7 skewers the same way. Arrange the skewers on a rimmed baking sheet and brush generously on all sides with olive oil. >>

Scallop Brochettes with Green Onions and Mango Salsa
(continued)

Oil the grill grate. Fold a footlong piece of aluminum foil in half lengthwise and lay it on the grill grate. Arrange the skewers so the exposed bamboo is protected from the flame by the foil and the food is directly over the medium-hot fire. Use 2 pieces of foil if necessary. Grill on one side until light grill marks appear on the scallops, about 3 minutes. Turn and grill until the scallops are etched with grill marks on the second side and are just opaque and cooked through in the center when tested with a knife, about 3 minutes longer.

Arrange 2 skewers on each warmed dinner plate, and drizzle the olive oil sauce over the skewers. Mound a spoonful of mango salsa alongside each pair of skewers. Serve immediately.

Mango Salsa

[MAKES ABOUT 2 CUPS]

1	TABLESPOON EXTRA-VIRGIN OLIVE OIL
½	TEASPOON GROUND CUMIN
½	TEASPOON GROUND CORIANDER
¼	TEASPOON KOSHER OR SEA SALT
2	LARGE, FIRM BUT RIPE MANGOES, PEELED, PITTED, AND CUT INTO ½-INCH DICE
¼	CUP FINELY DICED RED ONION
1	JALAPEÑO CHILE, SEEDED AND MINCED
¼	CUP CHOPPED FRESH CILANTRO
1	TABLESPOON FRESH LIME JUICE

In a small bowl, combine the olive oil, cumin, coriander, and salt and mix well.

In a medium bowl, combine the mangoes, onion, chile, cilantro, and lime juice. Add the oil mixture, stir to combine, and serve. This salsa tastes best if served within 8 hours, but it can be prepared up to 1 day in advance. Cover and refrigerate, then remove from the refrigerator 45 minutes before serving.

COOK'S NOTE Citrus-infused extra-virgin olive oils add big flavor to simply prepared foods, such as grilled steak, chicken, and vegetables, making the oils a staple in my grilling pantry. I buy them at specialty-foods stores, natural-foods stores, and Trader Joe's.

Garlic and Sea Salt Peel 'n' Eat Shrimp

Paired with a tall glass of beer or a salt-rimmed margarita, these shrimp make fantastic appetizers for casual entertaining. But eating with your fingers for dinner, especially with children, is always fun, too. Sometimes in summer, I'll set an outdoor table with a red-checkered cloth and paper plates for a family "beach" dinner featuring these big-flavored shrimp, lots of assorted crudités, corn on the cob, and some crusty rolls. Grill an extra 12 ounces shrimp and make Shrimp and Orzo Salad with Cherry Tomatoes, Green Onions, Feta, Kalamata Olives, and Lemon Vinaigrette (page 195) for another weeknight meal.

[SERVES 4]

3	LARGE CLOVES GARLIC
1	TABLESPOON SEA SALT
¼	CUP LOOSELY PACKED FRESH OREGANO LEAVES
½	CUP EXTRA-VIRGIN OLIVE OIL
2	POUNDS LARGE SHRIMP (26/30 COUNT) IN THE SHELL, DEVEINED

Prepare a medium-hot fire in a charcoal grill or preheat a gas grill on medium-high.

In a small food processor fitted with the metal blade, combine the garlic, salt, and oregano and process until minced. With the machine running, pour the olive oil through the feed tube and process until the marinade is well blended.

Reserve 2 tablespoons of the marinade for basting. In a bowl, toss the shrimp with the remaining marinade until well coated. Set aside while the grill heats.

Oil the grill grate. Remove the shrimp from the marinade and arrange them directly over the medium-hot fire. Grill, turning once, until the shrimp turn pink on the outside and are just opaque on the inside, about 2 minutes per side. Baste the shrimp with the reserved marinade as they grill. Transfer the shrimp to a serving bowl.

Let diners peel their own shrimp and enjoy the fun of eating with their fingers. Serve with plenty of napkins!

POULTRY

POULTRY ON THE GRILL   All of the recipes in this chapter, with the exception of the turkey burgers, call for either chicken or Cornish game hens. For weeknight grilling, I am using poultry that is readily available and fresh in the meat case. Even though duck, quail, and squab are well suited to grilling, I reserve those choices for times when I am entertaining. For the most part, I am using chicken parts, because the goal is quick weeknight meals. Chicken breasts and thighs are good candidates for simple marinades and rubs, but anyone who loves to nibble on bones and sweet charred edges shouldn't pass up grilled chicken wings.

The only way to grill a whole chicken and have it done in about a half hour or so is to butterfly, or spatchcock, it. The bird is cut along either side of the backbone and pressed open flat, cracking the rib bones in the process. It is easy to grill, serves four to six, and ideally there are leftovers. The challenge is to sear the outside without charring the skin and to cook the meat through at the same time. Game hens must be butterflied, as well, though they will cook in about half the time. Here are some additional tips, techniques, and guidelines for great grilled poultry.

FIRST, start with a clean, medium-hot, well-oiled grill surface. Even small bits of charred food left on the grill grate will stick to the raw poultry meat or skin, causing the flesh to tear when you try to the move the piece. Have the grill preheated; brush the grate so it's clean, clean, clean; and oil the grate thoroughly so it's well coated and slicked with oil.

SECOND, never put a cold piece of chicken on the grill. Remove the poultry from the refrigerator 20 to 30 minutes prior to grilling. Remove any clumps of fat and excess skin, as they will burn on the grill and cause flare-ups. If there is residual moisture on the meat, blot it dry with paper towels before marinating or using a dry rub. Some books direct you to rinse poultry, but I don't. Long ago, in a class taught by Craig Claiborne, a woman asked why he wasn't washing the poultry. His response made so much sense. He said, "Madame, exactly what germs are you killing by washing a chicken under cold running water, and how do you plan to sterilize the sink that you have just contaminated with the poultry juices?" I've never rinsed poultry since. Nowadays, the United States Food and Drug Administration advises against rinsing poultry, as well, explaining that proper cooking will kill any bacteria, and rinsing brings the possibility of splashing bacteria on countertops.

THIRD, with the exception of the skinless chicken breasts, chicken skewers, burgers, and pizza, all the recipes in this chapter are cooked in a covered grill using a two-zone fire (see page 21). The reason for this is control and timing. The best way to grill chicken, whether parts or a whole bird, is to sear it over a medium or medium-hot fire to create bronzed, caramelized, crisp skin, and then to finish it, covered, on the cool side of the grill, so the meat is cooked through but still moist and juicy.

FOURTH, even if the poultry has been seasoned with an oil-based marinade, paste, or rub before it goes on the grill, brush or spray it on all sides with oil. This technique is critical to successful poultry grilling. Don't be afraid to apply a good coating, especially on chicken breasts. It won't make the chicken oily, and it will prevent it from sticking.

FIFTH, use the right tools for moving and turning poultry. For breasts, thighs, wings, and even whole birds, I always use tongs, never a two-pronged fork, to move or turn the pieces, because a fork will pierce the flesh, allowing the juices to run out. If the skin is sticking to the grill grate, use a spatula to loosen it, being careful not to tear the skin.

SIXTH, use an instant-read thermometer to check doneness. Poultry is done when the internal temperature reaches 165°F. When grilling a whole chicken or Cornish hen, take the temperature in the thickest part of the thigh. Once the poultry is allowed to rest for 5 to 10 minutes, the carryover heat pushes the final temperature to about 170°F. The meat is moist and tender, cooked through, not pink at the bone, with a wonderfully seared, crisp-skinned exterior.

FINALLY, whole birds need to rest when they come off the grill. During cooking, the heat drives the juices into the cells and into the center of the meat. If you cut a whole chicken or Cornish hen the moment you take it off the grill, the juices will spill out on the carving board and the meat will be dry and less tender. If you allow the poultry to rest for 5 to 10 minutes before cutting into it, the juices will redistribute themselves evenly throughout the flesh, leaving the poultry juicy and tender when sliced.

Southwest Chipotle Chile–Grilled Chicken Breasts

The big, spicy, smoky flavors of this simple-to-put-together glaze turn ordinary grilled chicken breasts into a revved-up weeknight meal. Serve them whole, or slice them and pile the slices on warmed flour tortillas with sliced avocados and chopped tomatoes. Mix a generous tablespoon of minced canned chipotle chiles into 1/2 cup mayonnaise and you have an instant sauce for your tacos.

Double the recipe and reserve the leftovers to make Grilled Sweet Corn, Black Bean, and Cherry Tomato Salad with Southwest Chipotle Chile–Grilled Chicken (page 191), a bountiful main-course salad.

[SERVES 4]

4   TABLESPOONS (1/2 STICK) UNSALTED BUTTER
1/4 CUP HONEY
2   TABLESPOONS MINCED CANNED CHIPOTLE CHILES IN ADOBO SAUCE
1   TEASPOON KOSHER OR SEA SALT, PLUS MORE FOR SEASONING
4   BONELESS, SKIN-ON CHICKEN BREAST HALVES
    EXTRA-VIRGIN OLIVE OIL
    FRESHLY GROUND PEPPER

Prepare a medium-hot fire in a charcoal grill or preheat a gas grill on medium-high.

In a small saucepan or microwave-safe bowl, melt the butter. Add the honey, chiles, and 1 teaspoon salt and stir to mix thoroughly. Keep warm.

Generously brush the chicken breasts on both sides with olive oil and season with salt and pepper.

To create a cool zone, bank the coals to one side of the grill or turn off one of the burners. Oil the grill grate. Place the chicken breasts, skin side down, directly over the medium-hot fire and sear on one side, about 3 minutes. Turn and sear on the other side for 3 to 4 minutes. Move the chicken to the cooler part of the grill, and brush generously on both sides with the chipotle butter. Cover and grill, basting once or twice with more chipotle butter, until the juices run clear when the thickest part of a breast is pierced with a knife, or an instant-read thermometer registers 165°F, 6 to 8 minutes longer. Baste the chicken once or twice while it is grilling.

Divide the breasts among warmed dinner plates and serve immediately.

Chicken Breasts with Tarragon-Mustard Paste

This is my no-brainer weeknight grilled chicken meal. I use this same mustard paste on chicken thighs and wings. Whisk together the mustard mixture, slather it on the chicken breasts, and you're good to grill. There's even time, while the grill is getting hot, to make a salad. Middle Eastern Chickpea Salad (page 180) or Israeli Couscous with Zucchini, Red Bell Pepper, and Parsley (page 171) is a good choice.

[SERVES 4]

⅓ CUP DIJON MUSTARD

2 TABLESPOONS EXTRA-VIRGIN OLIVE OIL

1 TABLESPOON DRIED TARRAGON LEAVES, CRUSHED

½ TEASPOON FRESHLY GROUND PEPPER

4 BONELESS, SKIN-ON CHICKEN BREAST HALVES

Prepare a medium-hot fire in a charcoal grill or preheat a gas grill on medium-high.

In a bowl or baking dish large enough to hold the chicken, combine the mustard, olive oil, tarragon, and pepper. Stir to mix thoroughly. Add the chicken breasts and turn to coat on both sides. Set aside until the grill is ready.

To create a cool zone, bank the coals to one side of the grill or turn off one of the burners. Oil the grill grate. Place the chicken breasts, skin side down, directly over the medium-hot fire and sear on one side, about 5 minutes. Turn and sear on the other side for 5 minutes. Move the chicken breasts to the cooler part of the grill, cover, and grill until the juices run clear when the thickest part of a chicken breast is pierced with a knife, or an instant-read thermometer registers 165°F, 5 to 7 minutes longer.

Divide the chicken breasts among warmed plates. Serve immediately.

Garlic-Grilled Chicken
with Tomatillo Salsa and Tortillas

What's better for an easy dinner than grilled chicken stuffed inside warm tortillas and loaded with toppings? While the grill heats, I make a quick spice rub and prepare the chicken, and then I arrange all the toppings in serving bowls and set them on the table, ready for assembly. Skip the cilantro and avocado if you don't feel like chopping and slicing, and you can buy grated cheese as a time-saver. You can even use store-bought guacamole instead of the avocado. This meal lends itself to the whim of the cook.

[SERVES 4]

4   BONELESS, SKINLESS CHICKEN BREAST HALVES

1½ TABLESPOONS CHILI POWDER

1½ TEASPOONS GROUND TURMERIC

1½ TEASPOONS KOSHER OR SEA SALT

1   TEASPOON GARLIC POWDER

EXTRA-VIRGIN OLIVE OIL

1   LIME, QUARTERED

1   CUP LOOSELY PACKED FRESH CILANTRO LEAVES

2   LARGE HASS AVOCADOS, HALVED, PITTED, PEELED, AND CUT INTO THIN WEDGES

1½ CUPS (6 OUNCES) GRATED MONTEREY JACK CHEESE

2   CUPS SHREDDED ICEBERG LETTUCE

1½ CUPS STORE-BOUGHT TOMATILLO SALSA (SEE COOK'S NOTE, PAGE 79)

8   8-INCH FLOUR TORTILLAS

Prepare a medium-hot fire in a charcoal grill or preheat a gas grill on medium-high.

Remove any clumps of fat clinging to the chicken breasts and place the breasts in a shallow baking dish or bowl. In a small bowl, combine the chili powder, turmeric, salt, and garlic powder. Rub the chicken breasts on both sides with olive oil and then rub them with the spice rub. Set aside until the grill is ready.

Arrange the lime, cilantro, avocados, cheese, lettuce, and salsa in separate small bowls and have them ready for assembling the tacos.

Oil the grill grate. Place the chicken breasts directly over the medium-hot fire and sear on one side, about 4 minutes. Turn and sear on the other side until the juices run clear when the thickest part of a breast is pierced with a knife, or an instant-read thermometer registers

165°F, about 4 minutes longer. While the chicken is cooking, grill the tortillas. Depending on the size of the grill, lay 1 or 2 tortillas on the grill at a time, warming them over direct heat for about 15 seconds per side. Stack them on a plate and keep warm.

Transfer the chicken to a cutting board and cut across the grain into ¹/₂-inch-thick strips. Arrange on a warmed serving plate. Let diners assemble their own tacos. To assemble, place 2 chicken slices in a tortilla, squeeze a bit of lime juice over the chicken, and mound with cilantro, avocado, cheese, and lettuce. Spoon some salsa on top. Serve with plenty of napkins!

Cumin-Rubbed Chicken Breasts with Moroccan Pesto

Simple grilled chicken breasts are so satisfying and easy to prepare that I've included quite a few recipes in this chapter. For this recipe, a quick spice rub of ground cumin, salt, and pepper brings a flash of subtle grill flavor to the meat, but it's the final flourish of Moroccan Pesto that gives the dish its irresistible flavor. Serve with either Bulgur Salad with Smoky Grilled Tomatoes and Green Onions (page 174) or Middle Eastern Chickpea Salad (page 180).

[SERVES 4]

4   BONELESS, SKINLESS CHICKEN BREAST HALVES
2   TEASPOONS GROUND CUMIN
1½ TEASPOONS KOSHER OR SEA SALT
1½ TEASPOONS FRESHLY GROUND PEPPER
    EXTRA-VIRGIN OLIVE OIL
½   CUP MOROCCAN PESTO (PAGE 34)

Prepare a medium-hot fire in a charcoal grill or preheat a gas grill on medium-high.

Remove any pieces of fat clinging to the chicken breasts and place the breasts in a shallow baking dish or bowl. In a small bowl, combine the cumin, salt, and pepper. Rub the chicken breasts on both sides with olive oil and then rub them with the spice rub. Set aside until the grill is ready.

Oil the grill grate. Place the chicken breasts directly over the medium-hot fire and sear on one side, about 4 minutes. Turn and sear on the other side until the juices run clear when the thickest part of a breast is pierced with a knife, or an instant-read thermometer registers 165°F, about 4 minutes longer.

Divide the chicken breasts among warmed plates and drizzle with the pesto. Serve immediately.

Lemon-Marinated Chicken Breasts

Here's a way to grill once and get two easy weeknight meals. Start by buying enough boneless, skinless chicken breasts to feed the family for one night, and then throw an extra package of breasts into the grocery cart. At dinnertime, double the marinade recipe, marinate and grill all the chicken at once, and save four breast halves for making Hearts of Romaine Caesar Salad with Lemon-Marinated Chicken and Chunky Parmesan Croutons (page 193) on another night.

[SERVES 4]

¼   CUP EXTRA-VIRGIN OLIVE OIL
2   TABLESPOONS FRESH LEMON JUICE
2   LARGE CLOVES GARLIC, MINCED
¼   TEASPOON KOSHER OR SEA SALT
FRESHLY GROUND PEPPER
4   BONELESS, SKINLESS CHICKEN BREAST HALVES

Prepare a medium-hot fire in a charcoal grill or preheat a gas grill on medium-high.

In a bowl or baking dish large enough to hold the chicken, combine the olive oil, lemon juice, garlic, salt, and a few grinds of pepper, and stir to mix thoroughly. Add the chicken breasts and turn to coat on both sides. Let the chicken marinate while the grill heats.

Oil the grill grate. Place the chicken breasts directly over the medium-hot fire and sear on one side, about 4 minutes. Turn and sear on the other side until the juices run clear when the thickest part of a breast is pierced with a knife, or an instant-read thermometer registers 165°F, about 4 minutes longer.

Divide the chicken breasts among warmed dinner plates. Serve immediately.

Orange-and-Chipotle-Rubbed Chicken Breasts

A heady mix of chipotle chiles, orange juice, olive oil, garlic, and pepper adds a fruity-hot finish to grilled chicken breasts. Grill some slices of sweet onion, red bell pepper, and zucchini to serve with the chicken. A quick brush with extra-virgin olive oil and a sprinkle of salt and pepper are all the vegetables need.

[SERVES 4]

¼	CUP FRESH ORANGE JUICE
3	TABLESPOONS EXTRA-VIRGIN OLIVE OIL
2	TABLESPOONS MINCED CANNED CHIPOTLE CHILES IN ADOBO SAUCE
2	LARGE CLOVES GARLIC, MINCED
½	TEASPOON KOSHER OR SEA SALT
½	TEASPOON FRESHLY GROUND PEPPER
4	BONELESS, SKIN-ON CHICKEN BREAST HALVES

Prepare a medium-hot fire in a charcoal grill or preheat a gas grill on medium-high.

In a bowl or baking dish large enough to hold the chicken, combine the orange juice, olive oil, chiles, garlic, salt, and pepper. Stir to mix thoroughly. Add the chicken breasts and turn to coat on both sides. Let the chicken marinate while the grill heats.

To create a cool zone, bank the coals to one side of the grill or turn off one of the burners. Oil the grill grate. Place the chicken breasts, skin side down, directly over the medium-hot fire and sear on one side, about 3 minutes. Turn and sear on the other side for 3 to 4 minutes. Move the chicken to the cooler part of the grill, cover, and grill until the juices run clear when the thickest part of a breast is pierced with a knife, or an instant-read thermometer registers 165°F, 6 to 8 minutes longer.

Divide the chicken breasts among warmed dinner plates. Serve immediately.

Skewered Chicken Tenders Basted with Pesto Oil

Whether you have garden-fresh basil and make your own pesto or buy basil pesto at the grocery store, these chicken skewers will be quick and delicious. Serve them with Lemon Couscous with Dried Cranberries and Apricots (page 170) or a mixed grill of vegetables. Think of these skewers as party appetizers, too, or tote them cold for picnic fare. They are always a big hit with children.

[SERVES 4]

16 7-INCH BAMBOO SKEWERS, SOAKED IN WATER
FOR 15 MINUTES, THEN DRAINED (SEE PAGE 25)
¼ CUP STORE-BOUGHT BASIL PESTO,
AT ROOM TEMPERATURE
2 TABLESPOONS EXTRA-VIRGIN OLIVE OIL,
PLUS MORE FOR BRUSHING
1½ POUNDS CHICKEN BREAST TENDERS
(ABOUT 16 TENDERS)
KOSHER OR SEA SALT
FRESHLY GROUND PEPPER

Immerse the skewers before lighting the grill, so they have plenty of time to soak. Prepare a medium-hot fire in a charcoal grill or preheat a gas grill on medium-high.

In a small bowl, combine the pesto and 2 tablespoons olive oil and mix well; set aside. Place the chicken breast tenders in a bowl, drizzle olive oil over the top, and brush or rub the chicken on both sides with the oil. Season generously with salt and pepper.

Thread 1 chicken tender onto each skewer, unless there are small pieces to combine together. Weave the tenders so the skewers pierce each piece 2 or 3 times. Bunch the meat a bit, so it covers about 5 inches of the skewer.

Oil the grill grate. Fold a footlong piece of aluminum foil in half lengthwise and lay it on the grill grate. Arrange the skewers so the exposed bamboo is protected from the flame by the foil and the meat is directly over the fire. Use 2 pieces of foil if necessary. Grill the chicken, turning once and basting frequently with the pesto oil, until the meat is firm and the juices run clear when a tender is pierced with a knife, about 2½ minutes per side.

Divide the skewers among warmed dinner plates. Serve immediately.

Hoisin-Glazed Chicken Thighs

Here, a pared-down Asian basting sauce creates sweet, smoky, pungent flavors for meaty chicken thighs. The chicken is basted rather than marinated, so it doesn't burn on the grill from the sugar in the marinade. Searing the chicken first allows for the skin to crisp and color with nice grill marks before basting. Finishing the thighs, covered, on the cool side of the grill allows the smoky flavors and rich mahogany glaze to develop. Serve with steamed rice and Baby Bok Choy (page 147) or Asian-Style Eggplant (page 149).

[SERVES 4]

8   BONE-IN, SKIN-ON CHICKEN THIGHS
EXTRA-VIRGIN OLIVE OIL
KOSHER OR SEA SALT
FRESHLY GROUND PEPPER
1¼ CUPS HOISIN-GINGER BASTING SAUCE (PAGE 37)

Prepare a medium-hot fire in a charcoal grill or preheat a gas grill on medium-high.

Trim the chicken thighs of any excess skin and fat. Place the thighs in a large bowl, drizzle olive oil over the top, and brush or rub the thighs all over with the oil. Season generously with salt and pepper. Have the basting sauce in a bowl with a brush next to the grill.

To create a cool zone, bank the coals to one side of the grill or turn off one of the burners. Oil the grill grate. Place the chicken thighs, skin side down, directly over the medium-hot fire and sear on one side, about 3 minutes. Turn, baste with some of the sauce, and sear on the other side, about 7 minutes. Move the chicken to the cooler part of the grill, baste with more sauce, cover, and grill, basting the thighs twice more as they cook, until the juices run clear when the thickest part of a thigh is pierced with a knife, or an instant-read thermometer registers 165°F, 10 to 15 minutes longer.

Divide the chicken thighs among warmed dinner plates. Serve immediately.

Chicken Thighs with Espresso-Cardamom Rub

I first used this rub on pork chops, and then decided to try it with chicken thighs. I liked it so much—and it's so easy—that I decided to include the recipe. The versatility of this spice rub is another reason to have a well-stocked pantry for grilling. Serve the chicken with Walla Walla Sweet Onions (page 144) and Sweet Corn in the Husk (page 141).

8	BONE-IN, SKIN-ON CHICKEN THIGHS
[SERVES 4]	EXTRA-VIRGIN OLIVE OIL
⅓	CUP ESPRESSO-CARDAMOM RUB (PAGE 32)

Prepare a medium-hot fire in a charcoal grill or preheat a gas grill on medium-high.

Trim the chicken thighs of any excess skin and fat. Place the thighs in a large bowl, drizzle olive oil over the top, and brush or rub the thighs all over with the oil. Rub the thighs all over with the spice rub.

To create a cool zone, bank the coals to one side of the grill or turn off one of the burners. Oil the grill grate. Place the chicken thighs, skin side down, directly over the medium-hot fire and sear on one side, about 3 minutes. Turn and sear on the other side, about 7 minutes. Move the chicken to the cooler part of the grill, cover, and grill until the juices run clear when the thickest part of a thigh is pierced with a knife, or an instant-read thermometer registers 165°F, 10 to 15 minutes longer.

Divide the chicken thighs among warmed dinner plates. Serve immediately.

Chili-Rubbed Chicken Thighs with Smashed Grilled Potatoes and Mole Sauce

This weeknight dish doubles well as party fare. The combination of the smashed potatoes nestled between the electrifying mole sauce and grill-seared, chili-rubbed chicken thighs is wickedly delicious. The entire recipe can be doubled or even tripled for a crowd. The almost-from-scratch mole sauce is simple to make and doesn't need last-minute attention—just a reheat. I recommend making a big batch of the Grill Every Day Spice Rub (page 31) on a lazy weekend afternoon and keeping it on your pantry shelf. For entertaining, garnish the plates with fresh cilantro.

It's easy to juggle the cooking of the potatoes and chicken thighs. I arrange the potatoes on the cool side of the grill about 10 minutes after I start the grill, so they get a jump start on cooking. While the chicken thighs are searing and the lid of the grill is open, I turn the potatoes once, then I let them finish cooking along with the thighs when the thighs are moved to the cool side and the grill is covered. If you have a gas grill with more than two burners, you might need to turn off an additional burner to accommodate all of the food.

[SERVES 4]

8	BONE-IN, SKIN-ON CHICKEN THIGHS
	EXTRA-VIRGIN OLIVE OIL
1/3	CUP GRILL EVERY DAY SPICE RUB (PAGE 31)
1/4	CUP STORE-BOUGHT MOLE (SEE COOK'S NOTE, PAGE 124)
1	CUP CANNED LOW-SODIUM CHICKEN BROTH
1/4	TEASPOON GROUND CINNAMON
1/8	TEASPOON KOSHER OR SEA SALT
1/8	TEASPOON SUGAR
	GRILL-ROASTED AND SMASHED BABY WHITE POTATOES (PAGE 156)
1/3	CUP CHOPPED FRESH CILANTRO (OPTIONAL)

Prepare a medium-hot fire in a charcoal grill or preheat a gas grill on medium-high.

Trim the chicken thighs of any excess skin and fat. Place the thighs in a large bowl, drizzle olive oil over the top, and brush or rub the thighs all over with the oil. Rub the thighs all over with the spice rub. >>

Chili-Rubbed Chicken Thighs with Smashed Grilled Potatoes and Mole Sauce
(continued)

To create a cool zone, bank the coals to one side of the grill or turn off one of the burners. Oil the grill grate. Place the chicken thighs, skin side down, directly over the medium-hot fire and sear on one side, about 3 minutes. Turn and sear on the other side, about 7 minutes. Move the chicken to the cooler part of the grill, cover, and grill until the juices run clear when the thickest part of a thigh is pierced with a knife, or an instant-read thermometer registers 165°F, 10 to 15 minutes longer.

While the chicken is grilling, prepare the mole sauce. In a small saucepan, combine the mole, chicken broth, cinnamon, salt, and sugar and place over medium-low heat. Simmer, stirring occasionally, until the sauce is smooth and thickened, about 5 minutes. Keep warm.

To serve, spoon enough mole sauce on each dinner plate to cover the surface lightly. Arrange 2 or 3 smashed potatoes in the center of each plate, and set 2 chicken thighs on top. Garnish each plate with a generous sprinkling of cilantro. Serve immediately.

 COOK'S NOTE Mole sauce, such as Doña Maria brand, is available at Latin American markets, specialty-foods stores, and most supermarkets. Use this doctored sauce on everything from chicken enchiladas to sliced turkey.

Cornish Game Hens with Lemon Slices and Sage Leaves

This recipe, which calls for stuffing lemon slices and fresh sage leaves under the skin of game hens and then grilling them, reminds me of alfresco dining in Italy. Transport yourself with this family-friendly meal, or make these game hens for party-perfect entertaining. Choose a crisp white wine, such as an Orvieto or Soave. Grilled Polenta with Sweet Red Peppers and Onion Wedges (page 168) and Smoky Grill-Roasted Roma Tomatoes with Garlic (page 153) would make great accompaniments.

[SERVES 4]

4   CORNISH GAME HENS
2   LEMONS, ENDS TRIMMED, THINLY SLICED, AND SEEDS REMOVED
    (8 SLICES)
16 FRESH SAGE LEAVES
    EXTRA-VIRGIN OLIVE OIL
    KOSHER OR SEA SALT
    FRESHLY GROUND PEPPER

Prepare a medium fire in a charcoal grill or preheat a gas grill on medium.

To butterfly the hens, place a hen breast down on a cutting board. Using poultry shears, sharp, sturdy kitchen scissors, or a chef's knife, cut through the hen from one end to the other on each side of the backbone to remove it. Turn the hen breast side up, pull the body open, and use the heel of your hand to press down firmly, cracking the rib bones so the hen rests flat. Repeat with the other hens. Transfer to a large, rimmed baking sheet.

Using your fingers, and being careful not to tear the skin, loosen the skin from the breast of a hen to create a pocket. Slip 2 lemon slices under the skin, placing 1 slice over each breast half. Place 2 sage leaves on top of each lemon slice. Repeat with the other hens. Rub the hens generously on all sides with olive oil and season on all sides with salt and pepper.

To create a cool zone, bank the coals to one side of the grill or turn off one of the burners. Oil the grill grate. Place the hens, skin side down, directly over the medium fire, cover, and sear on one side, about 5 minutes. Turn, re-cover, and sear on the other side for about 5 minutes. Move the hens to the cooler part of the grill, cover, and grill until the juices run clear when the thickest part of the thigh is pierced with a knife, or an instant-read thermometer registers 165°F, 5 to 7 minutes longer.

Transfer to warmed dinner plates and let rest for 5 minutes before serving.

Butterflied Cornish Game Hens
with Garlic, Lemon, and Thyme Butter

Cornish game hens are a delight to grill, and they are quick enough for weeknight grilling because they are so petite. Plan ahead because game hens are usually sold frozen. This is a preparation with two steps: first, whip together a compound butter; second, butterfly the hens to remove the backbone and press them flat, so they are easy to grill. Add some vegetables and Sliced and Grilled Yukon Gold Potatoes (page 155), and a fabulous dinner is made.

[SERVES 4]

3 CLOVES GARLIC

ZEST OF 1 LEMON, REMOVED IN
   ½-INCH-WIDE STRIPS

1 TABLESPOON FRESH THYME LEAVES

KOSHER OR SEA SALT

FRESHLY GROUND PEPPER

½ CUP (1 STICK) UNSALTED BUTTER,
   AT ROOM TEMPERATURE, CUT INTO
   CHUNKS

4 CORNISH GAME HENS

Prepare a medium fire in a charcoal grill or preheat a gas grill on medium.

In a mini-chop or small food processor fitted with the metal blade, combine the garlic, lemon zest, thyme, and ½ teaspoon each salt and pepper and process until minced. Add the butter and process until well combined.

To butterfly the hens, place a hen, breast down, on a cutting board. Using poultry shears, sharp, sturdy kitchen scissors, or a chef's knife, cut through the hen from one end to the other on each side of the backbone to remove it. Turn the hen breast side up, pull the body open, and use the heel of your hand to press down firmly, cracking the rib bones so the hen rests flat. Repeat with the other hens. Transfer to a large, rimmed baking sheet.

Using your fingers, loosen the skin from the breast of a hen to create a pocket. Then, using about 2 tablespoons of the prepared butter, smear the butter all over the breast meat with your fingers, pushing some butter over the thigh meat. Repeat with the other hens. Rub all over with any remaining butter and season with salt and pepper.

To create a cool zone, bank the coals to one side of the grill or turn off one of the burners. Oil the grill grate. Place the hens, skin side down, directly over the medium fire, cover, and sear on one side, about 5 minutes. Turn, re-cover, and sear on the other side for about 5 minutes. Move the hens to the cooler part of the grill, re-cover, and grill until the juices run clear when the thickest part of the thigh is pierced with a knife, or an instant-read thermometer registers 165°F, 5 to 7 minutes longer.

Transfer the hens to warmed dinner plates and let rest for 5 minutes before serving.

Spatchcocked Chicken
with Blood Orange Oil and Fresh Herbs

Spatchcock, an old culinary term of Irish origin, is an abbreviation of "dispatch cock," a phrase used to describe preparing a bird by splitting it down the back, spreading it open like a book, and pressing it flat for easy, optimal grilling. I could have used the term "butterflied," as I did in the recipes for Cornish game hens, but it's fun to broaden our culinary lexicon, especially with a term this colorful.

For weeknight meals, spatchcocking the bird is the quickest way to get a whole chicken cooked and on the table. In addition, it is incredibly tasty because both the skin side and the bone side are exposed to the fire. I also use this technique (and recipe!) on rainy days when even I, an intrepid griller, decide to roast a chicken in a hot oven. When I was developing this recipe, I tried using the blood orange–infused olive oil in the mixture I spooned under the chicken skin, but I decided its delicate flavor was lost in the grilling. So, instead I use extra-virgin olive oil under the skin and save the more expensive blood orange oil for drizzling.

[SERVES 4]

3	TABLESPOONS EXTRA-VIRGIN OLIVE OIL, PLUS MORE FOR RUBBING
1	TABLESPOON MINCED FRESH THYME
1	TABLESPOON MINCED FRESH SAGE
1	TABLESPOON MINCED GARLIC
½	TEASPOON KOSHER OR SEA SALT, PLUS MORE FOR SEASONING
½	TEASPOON FRESHLY GROUND PEPPER, PLUS MORE FOR SEASONING
1	WHOLE CHICKEN, 3½ TO 4 POUNDS

BLOOD ORANGE–INFUSED EXTRA-VIRGIN OLIVE OIL
FOR DRIZZLING (SEE COOK'S NOTE, PAGE 106)
FLEUR DE SEL OR OTHER FINISHING SALT FOR SPRINKLING

Prepare a medium fire in a charcoal grill or preheat a gas grill on medium.

In a small bowl, combine the 3 tablespoons olive oil, the thyme, sage, garlic, and ½ teaspoon each kosher salt and pepper. Set aside.

To spatchcock the chicken, place the bird, breast down, on a cutting board. Using poultry shears, sharp sturdy kitchen scissors, or a chef's knife, cut through the chicken from one end to the other on each side of the backbone to remove it. Turn the chicken breast up, pull the body open, and use the heel of your hand to press down firmly, cracking the rib bones so the chicken rests flat. Transfer to a large, rimmed baking sheet.

Using your fingers, and being careful not to tear the skin, loosen the skin from the breast to create a pocket. Spoon the herb mixture under the skin, spreading it evenly over both sides of the breast. Rub the chicken generously on all sides with olive oil and season on all sides with kosher salt and pepper.

To create a cool zone, bank the coals to one side of the grill or turn off one of the burners. Oil the grill grate. Place the chicken, skin side down, directly over the medium fire, cover, and sear on one side, about 7 minutes. (Check halfway through the cooking time to make sure the skin isn't browning too quickly, and watch for flare-ups. Have a spray bottle of water near the grill to tame flare-ups.) Using long tongs or a spatula, turn the chicken and re-cover. Sear on the other side for 7 to 10 minutes. Move the chicken to the cooler part of the grill, re-cover, and grill until the juices run clear when the thickest part of the thigh is pierced with a knife, or an instant-read thermometer registers 165°F, about 15 minutes longer.

Transfer the chicken to a carving board and let rest for 5 to 10 minutes. Cut the chicken into parts for serving, slicing the breast meat, if desired. Drizzle the chicken with the blood orange olive oil and sprinkle with *fleur de sel*. Serve immediately.

Honey Mustard–Glazed Chicken Wings

What child (or adult) doesn't like eating with their fingers? Grilled chicken wings, especially ones coated with an herb-infused heady mustard paste, are divine when the skin gets crisp, slightly burnished at the edges, and bronzed from being grilled and basted over direct heat. Make the meal even more of a finger-licking delight by serving the wings with Sweet Corn in the Husk (page 141). A big salad, or even a bowlful of crudités with a creamy dressing for dipping, would make dinner complete.

[SERVES 4]

½ CUP HONEY MUSTARD
¼ CUP PLUS 3 TABLESPOONS EXTRA-VIRGIN OLIVE OIL
1 TABLESPOON DRIED TARRAGON, CRUSHED
½ TEASPOON FRESHLY GROUND PEPPER, PLUS MORE FOR SEASONING
16 CHICKEN WINGS (ABOUT 3¾ POUNDS)
KOSHER OR SEA SALT

Prepare a medium-hot fire in a charcoal grill or preheat a gas grill on medium-high.

In a small bowl, combine the mustard, ¼ cup of the olive oil, the tarragon, and ½ teaspoon pepper and mix well. Set aside.

Place the wings in a large bowl. Rub the wings all over with the 3 tablespoons olive oil and then season them lightly with salt and pepper.

Oil the grill grate. Place the chicken wings directly over the medium-hot fire and cover. Sear on one side, about 5 minutes. Turn, re-cover, and sear on the other side, about 5 minutes longer. Brush the wings all over with the mustard sauce and continue to grill, basting and turning the wings, until they are bronzed and the juices run clear when the thickest part of a wing is pierced with a knife, about 10 minutes longer.

Pile the wings on a warmed serving plate. Serve immediately.

Grilled Pizza with Barbecued Chicken, Cheddar, and White Onion Rings

There are three good reasons I like to cook pizza on a grill: First, I can get my grill hotter than my oven—600°F or a bit hotter, which is ideal for a crisp crust. Second, when I want pizza in the summer, firing up the grill rather than heating the oven keeps my kitchen cool. And third, it's fun!

Why not combine great barbecue flavor with vegetables and Cheddar cheese and put it on pizza? Use leftover chicken, or buy a rotisserie chicken and shred the breast meat. I don't specify a particular barbecue sauce, so use your favorite, keeping in mind that one with a kick of heat makes a particularly tasty pizza.

[MAKES ONE 14-INCH PIZZA; SERVES 4 TO 6]

- 1 16- TO 18-OUNCE PACKAGE FRESH OR FROZEN PIZZA DOUGH (SEE COOK'S NOTE, FACING PAGE)
- 2 CUPS SHREDDED ROAST CHICKEN BREAST
- ¾ CUP STORE-BOUGHT BARBECUE SAUCE
- ¾ CUP THINLY SLICED WHITE ONION
- 1 TABLESPOON MINCED GARLIC
- 1 RED BELL PEPPER, HALVED LENGTHWISE, SEEDED, DERIBBED, AND CUT INTO LONG, NARROW STRIPS
- 2 CUPS (8 OUNCES) COARSELY SHREDDED MEDIUM OR SHARP CHEDDAR CHEESE
- VEGETABLE-OIL COOKING SPRAY
- ALL-PURPOSE FLOUR FOR DUSTING
- ¼ CUP LIGHTLY PACKED FRESH CILANTRO LEAVES

If using fresh dough, remove it from the refrigerator 30 minutes before you roll it out. If using frozen dough, transfer it to the refrigerator a day before you plan to make pizza, so it can thaw slowly, and then let it sit at room temperature for 30 minutes before you roll it out.

Prepare a hot fire in a charcoal grill or preheat a gas grill on high. If the grill has a built-in thermometer, it should register between 500° and 600°F. Have ready a 14-inch, non-perforated pizza pan, preferably an inexpensive aluminum one.

While the grill heats, prepare the toppings: In a bowl, toss the chicken with ¼ cup of the barbecue sauce. Set aside. Have all the other toppings—onion, garlic, bell pepper, cheese—ready for assembly.

Coat the pizza pan with the vegetable-oil spray. Remove the dough from the plastic bag and place on a lightly floured work surface. Lightly dust the dough with flour. Using a rolling pin, roll the dough into a 10-inch round without rolling over the edges. Lift the dough occasionally to make sure it isn't sticking to the work surface. Shake the excess flour from the dough. Lay the dough on the prepared pizza pan and gently stretch it into a 14-inch round.

To top the pizza: Spread the remaining $\frac{1}{2}$ cup barbecue sauce over the dough, leaving a 1-inch border. Evenly scatter the onion, garlic, and red pepper over the sauce. Distribute the chicken over the vegetables, then top with the cheese.

Place the pizza in the center of the grill directly over the hot fire and cover. (Work quickly so the grill temperature doesn't drop too much.) Grill the pizza until the crust is crisp and golden brown, and the cheese is bubbly and melted, about 10 minutes.

Using a pizza peel or thick oven mitts, remove the pizza from the grill. Scatter the cilantro over the top. Cut the pizza into wedges and serve immediately.

COOK'S NOTE Pizza as a weeknight meal is possible with ready-made pizza dough, available either fresh (in the refrigerated case) or frozen in some grocery and specialty-foods stores. If, like me, you have a weakness for kitchen equipment, and you think you'll be making grilled pizza frequently, consider investing in a pizza stone made for the grill (see page 26). Follow the manufacturer's directions carefully, as the stone needs to be heated in the grill before the pizza is put on it.

Asian Turkey Burgers

Lean turkey burgers are a healthy alternative to traditional beef burgers. However, they can be pretty boring and bland without the addition of ingredients to pump up the flavor. I've chosen Asian flavors, loading the burgers with ginger, garlic, cilantro, green onions, and soy sauce. Turning them into cheeseburgers with a slice of provolone makes them even tastier. I have also dressed them up with mayonnaise flavored with soy sauce and lemon juice. This is an optional step, however; smearing the toasted buns with plain mayonnaise is fine, too.

[SERVES 4]

1½ POUNDS GROUND TURKEY

3 TABLESPOONS CHOPPED FRESH CILANTRO

2 GREEN ONIONS, INCLUDING 2 INCHES OF GREEN TOPS, VERY THINLY SLICED

2 TABLESPOONS PEELED AND MINCED FRESH GINGER

1 TABLESPOON MINCED GARLIC

3 TABLESPOONS LOW-SODIUM SOY SAUCE

2 TEASPOONS FRESH LEMON JUICE

½ TEASPOON KOSHER OR SEA SALT

2 TABLESPOONS CANOLA OIL

4 SLICES PROVOLONE CHEESE

4 SESAME-SEED HAMBURGER BUNS, SPLIT

4 LETTUCE LEAVES

SOY SAUCE MAYONNAISE (FACING PAGE; OPTIONAL)

Prepare a hot fire in a charcoal grill or preheat a gas grill on high.

In a large bowl, combine the turkey, cilantro, green onions, ginger, garlic, soy sauce, lemon juice, and salt and mix well. Divide into 4 equal portions, and shape each portion into a patty 1 inch thick. Refrigerate the patties while the grill heats.

Oil the grill grate. Brush the burgers on both sides with the canola oil. Place the burgers directly over the hot fire and sear on one side, about 5 minutes. Turn and sear on the other side until almost cooked through, about 4 minutes longer. Place a slice of cheese on each burger, cover the grill, and cook until the cheese is melted, about 1 minute longer. Place the buns, cut side down, on the grill to toast while the cheese is melting.

Serve the turkey burgers on the toasted buns with the lettuce and mayonnaise, if desired.

Soy Sauce Mayonnaise

[MAKES ½ CUP]

½ CUP MAYONNAISE
2 TEASPOONS LOW-SODIUM SOY SAUCE
1 TEASPOON FRESH LEMON JUICE

In a small bowl, mix together the mayonnaise, soy sauce, and lemon juice.
Cover and refrigerate until ready to serve.

VEGETABLES + VEGETARIAN MAIN COURSES

* CHERRY TOMATO SKEWERS WITH FRESH BASIL **138**

* ASPARAGUS SPEARS **140**

* SWEET CORN IN THE HUSK **141**

* MIXED GRILL OF ZUCCHINI AND YELLOW SUMMER SQUASH WITH PESTO OIL **143**

* WALLA WALLA SWEET ONIONS **144**

* BOURBON-AND-MAPLE-GRILLED ACORN SQUASH **145**

* BABY BOK CHOY **147**

* EGGPLANT WITH *HERBES DE PROVENCE* **148**

* ASIAN-STYLE EGGPLANT **149**

* EGGPLANT STACKS WITH FRESH MOZZARELLA AND BASIL THREADS ON A BED OF ARUGULA **150**

* QUICK-GRILLED RATATOUILLE **152**

* SMOKY GRILL-ROASTED ROMA TOMATOES WITH GARLIC **153**

* NEW POTATOES TOSSED WITH EXTRA-VIRGIN OLIVE OIL AND *FLEUR DE SEL* **154**

* SLICED AND GRILLED YUKON GOLD POTATOES **155**

* GRILL-ROASTED AND SMASHED BABY WHITE POTATOES **156**

* SLICED AND GRILLED GARNET SWEET POTATOES WITH HONEY AND ADOBO GLAZE **157**

* GRILLED SWEET ONION, THYME, AND WHITE FARMHOUSE CHEDDAR PIZZA **159**

* VERY VEGGIE GRILLED PIZZA WITH MARINATED ARTICHOKES **160**

* GRILLED TOFU WITH BABY BOK CHOY AND SWEET CHILE SAUCE **162**

* LEMONGRASS-GRILLED TOFU WITH THAI PEANUT SAUCE **164**

* PORTABELLA MUSHROOM BURGER WITH GRILLED ONIONS AND PESTO MAYONNAISE **165**

VEGETABLES ARE TRANSFORMED ON THE GRILL.
Their colors brighten, their flavors intensify, and their exterior crisps while their interior softens. In many instances, a brush with olive oil and a sprinkle of good salt are all that are needed, as the caramelizing and searing that happens over the fire adds plenty of flavor.

Almost all vegetables grill quickly, though they typically need to be cut to expose as much surface area as possible. Globe onions should be sliced into thick rounds, and eggplants and zucchini and other summer squashes benefit from being cut on a sharp diagonal or, in the case of small squashes, in half lengthwise. Cherry tomatoes work best on skewers, while potatoes should be either cut into slices for grilling over direct heat or left whole or halved for grill-roasting over indirect heat. Tofu needs to be drained and blotted dry, cut into thick slices, and then generously brushed with oil to prevent sticking. Here are some additional tips and techniques for grilling vegetables.

FIRST, start with a clean, hot or medium-hot, well-oiled grill surface. Even small bits of charred food left on the grill grate will stick to the raw vegetables, either tearing the flesh when you try to move them (the case with eggplant) or imparting an off flavor. Preheat the grill; brush the grate so it's clean, clean, clean; and oil the grate thoroughly so it's well coated and slick.

SECOND, never put cold vegetables on the grill. Remove the vegetables from the refrigerator 20 to 30 minutes prior to grilling. If there is residual moisture on the vegetables from washing them, blot them dry with paper towels before brushing with oil, marinating, or using a dry rub.

THIRD, use the right tools for turning vegetables. Use tongs, rather than a two-pronged fork, to move or turn them, for better control. For onions and other vegetables that risk falling apart, use a wide spatula. Some vegetables work best if you arrange them on a grill basket or grill grid (see page 26).

FINALLY, grilling extra vegetables is a great way to save time and have wonderfully flavored components for another meal. For example, extra grilled eggplants, onions, or peppers are good in pasta. Check out Chapter 9, The Grill Planner—Second Helpings, for loads of ideas for quick weeknight meals using grilled vegetables.

Cherry Tomato Skewers with Fresh Basil

When I was developing the recipe for Quick-Grilled Ratatouille (page 152), I tasted one of the cherry tomatoes hot off the grill and decided that skewered tomatoes with basil would make a quick, colorful side dish. I had extra tomatoes and basil on hand, and the grill was hot, so I threaded some skewers to put my idea to work! I grill the skewers over direct heat for only a minute so the basil leaves don't scorch, and then finish them in a cooler zone. For a fun appetizer for a party, serve the room-temperature skewers with a tiny ball *(bocconcino)* of fresh mozzarella threaded onto the end of each one.

8	7-INCH BAMBOO SKEWERS, SOAKED IN WATER FOR 15 MINUTES, THEN DRAINED (SEE PAGE 25)
40	CHERRY TOMATOES (ABOUT 1 PINT)
32	LARGE FRESH BASIL LEAVES
3	TABLESPOONS EXTRA-VIRGIN OLIVE OIL
	KOSHER OR SEA SALT
	FRESHLY GROUND PEPPER

[SERVES 4]

Immerse the skewers before lighting the grill, so they have plenty of time to soak. Prepare a medium-hot fire in a charcoal grill or preheat a gas grill on medium-high.

To assemble the skewers, thread 5 tomatoes onto each skewer, placing a basil leaf, folded in half crosswise, between the tomatoes. Arrange the skewers in a single layer on a rimmed baking sheet and brush the tomatoes generously on all sides with the olive oil.

To create a cool zone, bank the coals to one side of the grill or turn off one of the burners. Oil the grill grate. Place the skewers directly over the medium-hot fire and grill, turning once, until light grill marks appear on both sides, about 30 seconds per side. Move the skewers to the cooler part of the grill, cover, and grill until the tomatoes are hot but the skin hasn't blistered, 1 to 2 minutes longer.

Transfer the skewers to a serving platter and season with salt and pepper. Serve warm or at room temperature.

Asparagus Spears

I love the smoky sweetness that develops when asparagus is grilled. In fact, grilling is my favorite way to cook asparagus. Thick spears are a must. Pencil-thin spears tend to slip through the grill grate and, because they lack meatiness, can overcook and char in an instant. Don't forget to grill extra spears to use in other dishes, such as Grilled Asparagus Salad with Soft Poached Egg, Prosciutto, and Lemon-Parmesan Vinaigrette (page 184) or Composed Salad of Alder-Planked Salmon and Asparagus with Lemon Vinaigrette (page 189). Both of these main-course salads are a welcome centerpiece for a Sunday brunch or light supper.

[SERVES 4]

28   THICK ASPARAGUS SPEARS
1 TO 2 TABLESPOONS EXTRA-VIRGIN OLIVE OIL
KOSHER OR SEA SALT
FRESHLY GROUND PEPPER

Prepare a hot fire in a charcoal grill or preheat a gas grill on high.

Snap off the fibrous bottom end of each spear, or trim the whole bunch to a uniform length. If desired, using a vegetable peeler or sharp paring knife, peel the thick spears from slightly below the tip to the base. (This isn't a critical step; some cooks prefer their asparagus peeled, while others like them unpeeled.) Place the spears in a baking dish, toss them with the olive oil, and season lightly with salt and pepper.

Oil the grill grate. Place the asparagus directly over the hot fire and grill, turning several times, until grill marks appear on all sides and the spears are crisp-tender, about 4 minutes. (Timing will vary depending on the thickness of the spears.)

Transfer to a warmed platter and serve immediately.

Sweet Corn in the Husk

Smoky, grilled-in-the-husk kernels are unforgettable when served hot off the fire and smeared with softened butter. In the Cook's Note that follows, I give easy recipes for whipping up a chili butter and an herb butter. Both heighten the flavor of the corn and are fun to make when entertaining. I often double the butter recipes and put the leftovers in the refrigerator or freezer for another meal.

[SERVES 4]

4 EARS OF CORN, HUSKS INTACT
UNSALTED BUTTER, AT ROOM TEMPERATURE (SEE COOK'S NOTE)
KOSHER OR SEA SALT (OPTIONAL)
FRESHLY GROUND PEPPER (OPTIONAL)

Prepare a hot fire in a charcoal grill or preheat a gas grill on high.

Pull back the husk from each ear of corn without actually removing it. Remove the silk, and then re-cover the corn with the husk. Run water into the ears of corn, drain the excess, and then twist the husks at the top to close.

Oil the grill grate. Place the corn directly over the hot fire and grill, turning the ears several times to grill on all sides, until the husks are charred and the kernels are tender and lightly burnished, about 20 minutes.

Remove from the grill and pull back and discard the husks, or knot the pulled-back husks for a rustic-chic look. Generously brush the corn with butter and season with salt and pepper, if desired. Transfer to a warmed platter and serve hot.

COOK'S NOTE If you have time, make a quick chili butter or herb butter. For chili butter, combine 4 tablespoons (½ stick) softened unsalted butter with ½ teaspoon chili powder, a pinch of cayenne pepper, ½ teaspoon salt, ¼ teaspoon sugar, and 2 tablespoons minced fresh cilantro. For the herb butter, combine 4 tablespoons (½ stick) softened unsalted butter with 1 tablespoon minced fresh flat-leaf parsley, 1 tablespoon minced fresh tarragon, ½ teaspoon salt, and ¼ teaspoon sugar. Add freshly ground pepper, if desired.

Mixed Grill of Zucchini and Yellow Summer Squash with Pesto Oil

I tend to overbuy when the farmers' market is brimming with summer vegetables, especially all the delicate summer squashes. I especially can't resist the cute pattypans. For an attractive presentation, I slice the zucchini and yellow crookneck, straight neck, or cocozelle squashes on the diagonal, and cut the pattypan squashes horizontally so the slices look like flowers. Use this recipe as a guideline and mix and match whatever summer squashes look freshest in the market.

[SERVES 4]

2   TABLESPOONS STORE-BOUGHT BASIL PESTO
3   TABLESPOONS EXTRA-VIRGIN OLIVE OIL, PLUS MORE FOR BRUSHING
3   PATTYPAN OR OTHER YELLOW SUMMER SQUASHES, ENDS TRIMMED AND
    CUT INTO THICK SLICES (SEE HEADNOTE)
3   ZUCCHINI, ENDS TRIMMED AND CUT ON THE DIAGONAL INTO THICK SLICES
KOSHER OR SEA SALT
FRESHLY GROUND PEPPER

Prepare a hot fire in a charcoal grill or preheat a gas grill on high.

In a small bowl, combine the pesto and 3 tablespoons olive oil and mix well. Set aside.

Arrange the squash slices in a single layer on a large, rimmed baking sheet and brush generously on both sides with olive oil. Season with salt and pepper.

Oil the grill grate. Place the squash slices directly over the hot fire and grill, turning once, until dark brown grill marks appear and the slices are crisp-tender, 4 to 5 minutes.

Arrange the squash slices, overlapping them, on a warmed platter and drizzle the pesto oil over the top. Serve immediately.

Walla Walla Sweet Onions

I'm partial to Walla Walla sweet onions because I live in the Pacific Northwest and look forward to late June through early September, when they are in season. However, lots of wonderful varieties of sweet onions are grown around the country, and they turn up in markets at various times of the year. Look for Vidalia, Cuernavaca, Peru, or Maui sweet onions. Serve these grilled onions alone or as part of a mixed vegetable grill to accompany grilled steaks, lamb chops, pork, or poultry.

[SERVES 4]

2 LARGE WALLA WALLA OR OTHER SWEET ONIONS, CUT CROSSWISE INTO ½-INCH-THICK SLICES
⅓ CUP CANOLA OR GRAPESEED OIL
¾ TEASPOON GROUND CHIPOTLE CHILE
½ TEASPOON KOSHER OR SEA SALT

Prepare a hot fire in a charcoal grill or preheat a gas grill on high.

Arrange the onion slices in a single layer on a large, rimmed baking sheet. In a small bowl, combine the oil, chile, and salt and mix well. Brush both sides of each onion slice with the seasoned oil.

Oil the grill grate. Place the onions directly over the hot fire and grill, turning once, until grill marks appear on both sides and the onions are crisp-tender, about 4 minutes per side. (Use a combination of tongs and a long-handled spatula to turn the onion slices so they stay intact.)

Transfer to a warmed platter and serve hot, or keep warm until ready to serve.

Bourbon-and-Maple-Grilled Acorn Squash

In late summer, when winter squashes start to appear in the farmers' market, I think about all the soups and stews I like to make, but I also think about how much I like squash on the grill. I prefer to grill-roast acorn squash instead of other varieties because it cuts so easily into neat wedges. Butternut or delicata squashes work well on the grill, too, but they need to be cut into thick slices. Although slices can be generously brushed with the bourbon butter, the curve of a wedge nicely captures a pool of glaze that beautifully burnishes the surface. Grilled squash complements pork and poultry, especially Spatchcocked Chicken with Blood Orange Oil and Fresh Herbs (page 128).

	¾ CUP (1½ STICKS) UNSALTED BUTTER
	¼ CUP PURE MAPLE SYRUP
	¼ CUP PACKED DARK BROWN SUGAR
[SERVES 4]	1 TEASPOON KOSHER OR SEA SALT, PLUS MORE FOR SPRINKLING
	1 TEASPOON FRESHLY GROUND PEPPER
	¼ CUP GOOD-QUALITY BOURBON WHISKEY SUCH AS MAKER'S MARK
	2 ACORN SQUASHES

Prepare a medium-hot fire in a charcoal grill or preheat a gas grill on medium-high.

In a small saucepan, melt the butter over medium heat. Pour or ladle ¼ cup of the butter into a heatproof bowl or measuring cup and set aside. Add the maple syrup, brown sugar, 1 teaspoon salt, and the pepper to the butter in the pan and whisk until the sugar is melted. Remove from the heat, add the bourbon, and stir until smooth. Set aside and keep warm.

Cut each squash in half lengthwise. Scoop out and discard the seeds and strings. Cut each half into thick wedges, either thirds or quarters, depending on the size of the squash. Arrange the squash in a single layer on a rimmed baking sheet and brush the wedges generously on the flesh side with the reserved melted butter. Sprinkle with salt.

To create a cool zone, bank the coals to one side of the grill or turn off one of the burners. Oil the grill grate. Place the squash on the cool side of the grill, cover, and grill until just beginning to caramelize at the edges and soften, 15 minutes. Brush the wedges with the bourbon-butter mixture, re-cover, and grill an additional 5 minutes. Brush the wedges again, re-cover, and grill until tender when pierced with a knife, about 5 minutes longer.

Transfer the squash wedges to a serving platter and serve immediately, or keep warm until ready to serve.

Baby Bok Choy

While writing this book, I tried grilling all sorts of vegetables, some more successfully than others. Baby bok choy was a surprise, because I thought it might be too delicate. But with a little care, it grills beautifully. The lower portion of the white stalks can be positioned directly over the fire, but you need to protect the tender green leaves from scorching by laying them on a long strip of foil. If you have a round, kettle-style grill, use two long foil strips and grill the bok choy in two rows. If you have a rectangular grill, use one long foil strip and grill them in a single row. In either case, you may need to cook these greens in two batches. They taste great drizzled with peanut sauce. I've sampled many brands, and House of Tsang is my favorite.

[SERVES 4]

8   HEADS BABY BOK CHOY, HALVED LENGTHWISE
2   TABLESPOONS CANOLA OR GRAPESEED OIL
2   TEASPOONS ASIAN SESAME OIL
KOSHER OR SEA SALT
STORE-BOUGHT THAI PEANUT SAUCE FOR DRIZZLING

Prepare a medium-hot fire in a charcoal grill or preheat a gas grill on medium-high.

Arrange the bok choy in a single layer on a large, rimmed baking sheet. In a small bowl, combine the canola and sesame oils and mix well. Brush both sides of the crisp white stalks (not the green leaves) of the bok choy with the oil mixture. Season the stalks lightly with salt.

Oil the grill grate. Place a long strip of foil, about 6 inches wide, across the length of the grill. Arrange the bok choy, cut side down, so the white stalks are directly over the medium-hot fire and the delicate green leaves are resting on the foil, protected from the fire. Grill until light brown grill marks appear, about $1\frac{1}{2}$ minutes. Turn and grill until light brown grill marks appear and the bok choy is crisp-tender when pierced with a knife, about 2 minutes longer.

Arrange the bok choy halves, cut side up, on a warmed platter and drizzle with the peanut sauce. Serve immediately.

Eggplant with *Herbes de Provence*

This is a simple and tasty way to prepare eggplants, with the bit of char that develops at the skin's edge contributing to the overall meaty, sweet flavor. I use any leftovers for sandwiches, such as a crusty baguette smeared with herbed goat cheese and layered with grilled eggplant and sliced onions and tomatoes.

2	PURPLE GLOBE EGGPLANTS (ABOUT 12 OUNCES EACH), CUT CROSSWISE INTO ½-INCH-THICK SLICES
½	CUP EXTRA-VIRGIN OLIVE OIL
1	TABLESPOON *HERBES DE PROVENCE*, CRUSHED
1	TEASPOON KOSHER OR SEA SALT

[SERVES 4]

Prepare a medium-hot fire in a charcoal grill or preheat a gas grill on medium-high.

Arrange the eggplant slices in a single layer on a large, rimmed baking sheet. In a small bowl, combine the olive oil, *herbes de Provence*, and salt and mix well. Generously brush the eggplant slices on both sides with the oil mixture.

Oil the grill grate. Place the eggplant slices directly over the medium-hot fire, cover, and grill until dark brown grill marks appear, 2 to 3 minutes. Turn, re-cover, and grill until dark grill marks appear and the slices are tender when pierced with a knife, about 3 minutes longer.

Transfer to a warmed serving plate and serve immediately, or keep warm until ready to serve.

Asian-Style Eggplant

Narrow and straight Asian (or Japanese) eggplants cook up tender and sweet, especially when grilled. I usually see the dark purple variety in the market, but on occasion striated purple or ivory eggplants are available, and all of them are delicious grilled. I created this quick sauce as an accompaniment to grilled eggplant, but know that a drizzle of soy sauce and Asian sesame oil is equally good. Make the sauce if you have time. (I use the same sauce as a dressing for a salad of shelled *edamame* and sliced celery—easy, crisp, and healthy.)

	¼	CUP MAYONNAISE
	1	TABLESPOON WHITE MISO (SEE COOK'S NOTE, PAGE 73)
MISO MAYONNAISE	1½	TEASPOONS ASIAN SESAME OIL
	1	TEASPOON SOY SAUCE
	¼	TEASPOON FRESHLY GROUND WHITE PEPPER
	4	PURPLE ASIAN EGGPLANTS (ABOUT 8 INCHES LONG), STEM ENDS TRIMMED, HALVED LENGTHWISE
[SERVES 4]	5	TABLESPOONS CANOLA OR GRAPESEED OIL
	2	TABLESPOONS ASIAN SESAME OIL
		KOSHER OR SEA SALT

Prepare a medium-hot fire in a charcoal grill or preheat a gas grill on medium-high.

Make the miso mayonnaise: In a small bowl, whisk together the mayonnaise, miso, sesame oil, soy sauce, and pepper until well blended. Set aside.

Arrange the eggplant halves in a single layer on a large, rimmed baking sheet. In a small bowl, stir together the canola and sesame oils. Generously brush both sides of each eggplant half with the oil mixture. Season the flesh sides lightly with salt.

Oil the grill grate. Place the eggplants, flesh side down, directly over the medium-hot fire. Cover and grill until dark brown grill marks appear, about 3 minutes. Turn, re-cover, and grill on the skin side until the eggplants are tender when pierced with a knife, about 3 minutes longer.

Arrange the eggplant halves, flesh side up, on a warmed platter. Drizzle the sauce over the top, or pass the sauce at the table. Serve immediately, or keep warm until ready to serve.

Eggplant Stacks with Fresh Mozzarella and Basil Threads on a Bed of Arugula

For a light summer meal, this is my kind of eating! Top smoky-grilled eggplant slices with fresh mozzarella, let the cheese get hot and oozy from the heat of the covered grill, and then serve the "stacks" over garden-fresh arugula, which will gently wilt from the heat of the eggplant. A drizzle of peppery Tuscan olive oil, a little freshly ground pepper, and a chiffonade of basil complement all the flavors. I developed this vegetarian main course for my college-age daughter, but if you eat meat, I recommend you lay two slices of prosciutto over the arugula before you top it with the eggplant stack. And in smaller portions, these stacks make great appetizers, with or without the prosciutto.

[SERVES 4]

1	LARGE PURPLE GLOBE EGGPLANT (ABOUT 1 POUND), CUT CROSSWISE INTO 8 THICK SLICES
3	TABLESPOONS TUSCAN EXTRA-VIRGIN OLIVE OIL, PLUS MORE FOR DRIZZLING
	KOSHER OR SEA SALT
2	LARGE BALLS (8 OUNCES TOTAL) FRESH MOZZARELLA CHEESE, EACH CUT INTO 4 SLICES
4	OUNCES ARUGULA
6	LARGE FRESH BASIL LEAVES, STACKED, ROLLED LIKE A CIGAR, AND CUT CROSSWISE INTO FINE THREADS
	FRESHLY GROUND PEPPER

Prepare a medium-hot fire in a charcoal grill or preheat a gas grill on medium-high.

Arrange the eggplant slices in a single layer on a large, rimmed baking sheet and brush the slices on both sides with the 3 tablespoons olive oil. Sprinkle with salt.

Oil the grill grate. Arrange the eggplant directly over the medium-hot fire, cover, and grill until dark brown grill marks appear, 2 to 3 minutes. Turn, re-cover, and grill until dark grill marks appear, about 2 minutes longer. Place a slice of mozzarella on top of each eggplant slice, re-cover, and grill until the eggplant is tender when pierced with a knife and the cheese is hot and melted, about 3 minutes longer.

To serve, place one-fourth of the arugula in the center of each warmed dinner plate. Top with 2 eggplant slices, overlapping them slightly. Scatter the basil threads over the top. Drizzle about 1 tablespoon olive oil over the top of each serving, and garnish with pepper. Serve immediately.

Quick-Grilled Ratatouille

What is traditionally a slow-braised French vegetable dish cooked in layers turns into a fabulous summer vegetable stew when the vegetables are grilled until crisp-tender and then chopped and mixed with fresh basil and tomato sauce. The smoky flavors of the grilled vegetables meld and accent one another. Serve alongside grilled beef, pork, chicken, or especially lamb.

[SERVES 4 TO 6]

2   10-INCH BAMBOO SKEWERS, SOAKED IN WATER FOR 15 MINUTES, THEN DRAINED (SEE PAGE 25)

⅓ CUP ROASTED GARLIC–FLAVORED OLIVE OIL

1½ TABLESPOONS *HERBES DE PROVENCE*, CRUSHED

½ TEASPOON KOSHER OR SEA SALT, PLUS MORE FOR SEASONING

½ PINT CHERRY TOMATOES

1   LARGE PURPLE GLOBE EGGPLANT (ABOUT 1 POUND), STEM END TRIMMED, CUT LENGTH-WISE INTO ¾-INCH-THICK SLICES

2   ZUCCHINI, ENDS TRIMMED, HALVED LENGTHWISE

1   LARGE RED BELL PEPPER, QUARTERED LENGTHWISE, SEEDED, AND DERIBBED

1   WALLA WALLA OR OTHER SWEET ONION, CUT CROSSWISE INTO ½-INCH-THICK SLICES

10 LARGE FRESH BASIL LEAVES, COARSELY CHOPPED

1   TABLESPOON TOMATO PASTE

FRESHLY GROUND PEPPER

Immerse the skewers before lighting the grill, so they have plenty of time to soak. Prepare a medium-hot fire in a charcoal grill or preheat a gas grill on medium-high.

In a small bowl, combine the olive oil, *herbes de Provence*, and ½ teaspoon salt and mix well. Thread the tomatoes onto the skewers and arrange on a plate. Brush the tomatoes lightly with the oil mixture. Arrange the remaining vegetables in a single layer on a large, rimmed baking sheet and brush generously on both sides with the oil mixture.

Oil the grill grate. Place all the vegetables except the tomatoes directly over the medium-hot fire, and grill, turning once, until dark brown grill marks appear on both sides and the vegetables are crisp-tender when pierced with a knife, 2 to 3 minutes per side. Timing will vary slightly for each vegetable; watch carefully and turn the vegetables as needed. Grill the skewered tomatoes at the same time, turning them before their skin blisters, about 2 minutes total.

Transfer the grilled vegetables except the tomatoes to a cutting board, and cut into ½-inch chunks. Place in a large bowl. Slide the tomatoes off the skewers and add to the vegetables in the bowl, along with the basil. Mix the tomato paste with 2 tablespoons water to thin it, and fold the diluted paste evenly into the vegetable mixture. Season to taste with salt and pepper. Serve warm or at room temperature.

Smoky Grill-Roasted Roma Tomatoes with Garlic

Tomatoes are so delicate to grill that I tried grilling them on a bed of herbs for two reasons: one, to protect them from the direct flame but still achieve a bit of charring; and two, to infuse them with an herbal flavor from the smoking rosemary. The method proved highly successful! Pick tomatoes that are firm but ripe. I used Roma tomatoes, but choose what looks good in the market. If you use a larger beefsteak or heirloom tomato, double the oil mixture, since you will have more surface area to brush. Grill extra tomatoes and make Bulgur Salad with Smoky Grilled Tomatoes and Green Onions (page 174).

[SERVES 4]

8	4-INCH-LONG SPRIGS FRESH ROSEMARY
2	TABLESPOONS ROASTED GARLIC-FLAVORED OLIVE OIL, PLUS MORE FOR BRUSHING
2	TEASPOONS MINCED FRESH BASIL
1	TEASPOON MINCED GARLIC
¼	TEASPOON KOSHER OR SEA SALT
¼	TEASPOON FRESHLY GROUND PEPPER
4	ROMA TOMATOES, HALVED CROSSWISE

Prepare a medium fire in a charcoal grill or preheat a gas grill on medium.

Run water over the rosemary sprigs to dampen them. Set aside. In a small bowl, combine the 2 tablespoons garlic-flavored olive oil, basil, garlic, salt, and pepper. Set aside. Arrange the tomatoes, cut side up, on a rimmed baking sheet or a plate and brush the cut side of each tomato with the olive oil mixture.

Oil the grill grate. Arrange the rosemary sprigs in a row, perpendicular to the bars of the grill grate and slightly separated, directly over the medium fire. Place the tomatoes, cut side down, on top of the rosemary. Cover and grill until tender but firm, about 3 minutes. Using tongs, gently turn the tomatoes cut side up, and brush off any of the charred rosemary leaves. Brush the tomatoes generously with the olive oil mixture. Cover and grill until the tomatoes are juicy and tender but still hold their shape, about 2 minutes longer.

Transfer to a warmed serving platter or individual dinner plates and serve immediately, or keep warm until ready to serve.

New Potatoes Tossed with Extra-Virgin Olive Oil and *Fleur de Sel*

Grilling lends an appealing smoky flavor to potatoes that cannot be achieved with any other cooking method. A final drizzle of a peppery Tuscan olive oil and a sprinkling of coarse French sea salt is my favorite way to serve them. I always grill extra and use them to make salmon hash, or I slice them for a quick meal of home fries and eggs.

[SERVES 4]

1 TO 1¼ POUNDS NEW RED POTATOES, HALVED

2   TABLESPOONS TUSCAN EXTRA-VIRGIN OLIVE OIL,
     PLUS MORE FOR DRIZZLING

KOSHER OR SEA SALT

FRESHLY GROUND PEPPER

FLEUR DE SEL FOR SPRINKLING

Prepare a medium-hot fire in a charcoal grill or preheat a gas grill on medium-high.

Poke the potato halves once with the tines of a fork. Place the potatoes in a bowl and toss them with the 2 tablespoons olive oil. Season lightly with salt and pepper.

To create a cool zone, bank the coals to one side of the grill or turn off one of the burners. Oil the grill grate. Arrange the potatoes, cut side down, directly over the medium-hot fire, cover, and grill until dark brown grill marks appear, about 4 minutes. Turn cut side up, re-cover, and grill for 4 minutes longer. Move the potatoes to the cooler part of the grill, cover, and grill until tender when pierced with a knife, about 10 minutes longer.

Transfer the potatoes to a serving bowl. Drizzle with olive oil, sprinkle with *fleur de sel*, and toss. Serve immediately, or keep warm until ready to serve.

Sliced and Grilled Yukon Gold Potatoes

I've included three potato recipes because the popular tubers are easy to grill, and because each recipe reflects a slightly different grilling technique, depending on the size and variety of potato. For Yukon Gold potatoes, which have a rich flavor, buttery texture, and lovely golden hue, grilling thick slices directly over the fire locks in the creamy richness and creates a crisp outer crust. I often pair this dish with Skirt Steak, Argentine Style (page 48) or with Hanger Steaks with Chile-Rubbed Grilled Onions (page 50).

[SERVES 4]

4 YUKON GOLD POTATOES (ABOUT 2 POUNDS), CUT INTO ½-INCH-THICK SLICES

¼ CUP EXTRA-VIRGIN OLIVE OIL, PLUS MORE FOR DRIZZLING

KOSHER OR SEA SALT

FRESHLY GROUND PEPPER

FLEUR DE SEL OR OTHER FINISHING SALT FOR SPRINKLING

Prepare a medium fire in a charcoal grill or preheat a gas grill on medium.

Arrange the potato slices in a single layer on a large, rimmed baking sheet and brush both sides of each slice generously with the ¼ cup olive oil. Season with kosher salt and pepper.

Oil the grill grate. Place the potatoes directly over the medium fire, cover, and grill until dark brown grill marks appear, about 4 minutes. Turn, re-cover, and grill until dark grill marks appear and the potatoes are tender when pierced with a knife, about 4 minutes longer.

Transfer to a serving platter, drizzle with a little olive oil, and sprinkle with *fleur de sel*. Serve immediately, or keep warm until ready to serve.

Grill-Roasted and Smashed Baby White Potatoes

No side dish is simpler to prepare than this one. Serve these potatoes as an easy accompaniment to almost any of the beef, lamb, poultry, or pork recipes in this book, especially ones with a sauce. One of my favorites is Chili-Rubbed Chicken Thighs with Smashed Grilled Potatoes and Mole Sauce (page 122).

[SERVES 4]

1 TO 1¼ POUNDS BABY WHITE POTATOES (CREAMERS)

2 TABLESPOONS EXTRA-VIRGIN OLIVE OIL

KOSHER OR SEA SALT

FRESHLY GROUND PEPPER

Prepare a medium-hot fire in a charcoal grill or preheat a gas grill on medium-high.

Poke the potatoes in several places with the tines of a fork. Place the potatoes in a bowl and toss them with the olive oil. Season with salt and pepper.

To create a cool zone, bank the coals to one side of the grill or turn off one of the burners. Oil the grill grate. Arrange the potatoes in a single layer on the cool side of the grill, cover, and grill until tender when pierced with a knife, 18 to 20 minutes.

Transfer to a cutting board. Using the side of a chef's knife or a wide spatula, press down on each potato until it is lightly smashed. Transfer to a warmed serving platter and serve immediately, or keep warm until ready to serve.

Sliced and Grilled Garnet Sweet Potatoes
with Honey and Adobo Glaze

Whether labeled "yam" or "sweet potato" in the market, the Garnet, with its garnet skin and orangey yellow flesh, is the best sweet potato for grilling. Look for firm, unblemished potatoes that are fairly uniform in size, so all the slices are about the same diameter. Pair the Garnets with Latin-Rubbed Pork Tenderloin (page 66), Espresso-Cardamom-Rubbed Pork Chops (page 76), or Orange-and-Chipotle-Rubbed Chicken Breasts (page 117).

[SERVES 4]

6 TABLESPOONS (¾ STICK) UNSALTED BUTTER

3 TABLESPOONS HONEY

1 TABLESPOON ADOBO SAUCE FROM CANNED CHIPOTLE CHILES

2 POUNDS GARNET SWEET POTATOES, PEELED AND CUT ON THE DIAGONAL INTO ½-INCH-THICK SLICES

KOSHER OR SEA SALT

Prepare a medium fire in a charcoal grill or preheat a gas grill on medium.

In a small saucepan, melt the butter over medium heat. Pour or ladle 3 tablespoons of the butter into a small heatproof bowl or measuring cup. Set aside. Add the honey and adobo sauce to the butter in the pan and whisk until smooth. Set aside and keep warm.

Arrange the potato slices in a single layer on a large, rimmed baking sheet, and brush the slices on both sides with the reserved melted butter. Sprinkle with salt.

To create a cool zone, bank the coals to one side of the grill or turn off one of the burners. Oil the grill grate. Arrange the potatoes directly over the medium fire, cover, and grill until dark brown grill marks appear, about 3 minutes. Turn, re-cover, and grill until dark grill marks appear, about 3 minutes longer. Move the potatoes to the cooler part of the grill, brush generously on both sides with the honey–butter mixture, re-cover, and grill until the potatoes are tender when pierced with a knife, 3 to 5 minutes longer.

Transfer the potatoes to a warmed platter and brush with any remaining glaze. Serve immediately, or keep warm until ready to serve.

Grilled Sweet Onion, Thyme, and White Farmhouse Cheddar Pizza

I grill sweet onions, especially the Walla Walla variety, from the moment they arrive in the market. Of course, they're great served as hunky slices on top of a grilled burger or steak, but nothing beats grilled sweet onions scattered over a pizza crust, especially when a white farmhouse Cheddar is melted on top. Visually, this is a beautiful white pizza, with the flecks of fresh thyme giving it a pop of color.

[MAKES ONE 14-INCH PIZZA; SERVES 4 TO 6]

- 1 16- TO 18-OUNCE PACKAGE FRESH OR FROZEN PIZZA DOUGH (SEE COOK'S NOTE, PAGE 133)
- 1 LARGE WALLA WALLA OR OTHER SWEET ONION, CUT CROSSWISE INTO ¼-INCH-THICK SLICES
- EXTRA-VIRGIN OLIVE OIL
- VEGETABLE-OIL COOKING SPRAY
- ALL-PURPOSE FLOUR FOR DUSTING
- 1 TABLESPOON FRESH THYME LEAVES
- FRESHLY GROUND PEPPER
- 6 OUNCES WHITE FARMHOUSE CHEDDAR CHEESE, THINLY SLICED

If using fresh dough, remove it from the refrigerator 30 minutes before you roll it out. If using frozen dough, transfer it to the refrigerator a day before you plan to make pizza, so it can thaw slowly, and then let it sit at room temperature for 30 minutes before you roll it out.

Prepare a hot fire in a charcoal grill or preheat a gas grill on high. If the grill has a built-in thermometer, it should register between 500° and 600°F. Have ready a 14-inch, non-perforated pizza pan, preferably an inexpensive aluminum one.

While the grill is heating, arrange the onion slices in a single layer on a large, rimmed baking sheet and brush the slices on both sides with olive oil. Set aside.

Oil the grill grate. Place the onions directly over the hot fire and grill, turning once, until grill marks appear on both sides and the onions are crisp-tender when pierced with a knife, about 4 minutes per side. (Use a combination of tongs and a long-handled spatula to turn the onion slices so they stay intact.) Set aside.

Coat the pizza pan with vegetable-oil spray. Remove the dough from the plastic bag and place on a lightly floured work surface. Lightly dust the dough with flour. Using a rolling pin, roll the dough into a 10-inch round without rolling over the edges. Lift the dough occasionally to make sure it isn't sticking to the work surface. Shake the excess flour from the dough. Lay the dough on the prepared pizza pan and gently stretch it into a 14-inch round. >>

Grilled Sweet Onion, Thyme, and White Farmhouse Cheddar Pizza
(continued)

To top the pizza: Brush olive oil over the crust, leaving a 1-inch border. Separate the onion slices into rings and arrange evenly over the pizza dough. Scatter the thyme over the top and season with a few grinds of pepper. Evenly distribute the cheese over the onions.

Place the pizza in the center of the grill directly over the hot fire and cover. (Work quickly so the grill temperature doesn't drop too much.) Grill the pizza until the crust is crisp and golden brown and the cheese is bubbly and melted, about 10 minutes.

Using a pizza peel or thick oven mitts, remove the pizza from the grill. Slice the pizza into wedges and serve immediately.

Very Veggie Grilled Pizza with Marinated Artichokes

First, I packed this pizza with colorful vegetables that I tossed with extra-virgin olive oil, fresh oregano, and red pepper flakes for a flavor boost. Then, to make the pie even more irresistible to the vegetable lover, I added tomatoes, artichokes, and olives. Finally, I added a mountain of grated mozzarella, for a meltingly delicious vegetarian meal.

[MAKES ONE
14-INCH PIZZA;
SERVES 4 TO 6]

1	16- TO 18-OUNCE PACKAGE FRESH OR FROZEN PIZZA DOUGH (SEE COOK'S NOTE, PAGE 133)
½	SMALL WALLA WALLA OR OTHER SWEET ONION, CUT INTO THIN WEDGES
1	SMALL YELLOW OR RED BELL PEPPER, HALVED LENGTHWISE, SEEDED, DERIBBED, AND CUT INTO LONG, NARROW STRIPS
1	LARGE CLOVE GARLIC, MINCED
2	TABLESPOONS EXTRA-VIRGIN OLIVE OIL
1	TABLESPOON CHOPPED FRESH OREGANO
½	TEASPOON RED PEPPER FLAKES
¼	TEASPOON KOSHER OR SEA SALT
	VEGETABLE-OIL COOKING SPRAY
	ALL-PURPOSE FLOUR FOR DUSTING
¼	CUP STORE-BOUGHT MARINARA SAUCE
1	JAR (6 OUNCES) MARINATED ARTICHOKE HEARTS, WELL DRAINED AND HALVED
2	PLUM TOMATOES, CORED AND THINLY SLICED
⅓	CUP PITTED AND HALVED CANNED RIPE OLIVES
2	CUPS (8 OUNCES) COARSELY SHREDDED WHOLE-MILK OR PART-SKIM, LOW-MOISTURE MOZZARELLA CHEESE

If using fresh dough, remove it from the refrigerator 30 minutes before you roll it out. If using frozen dough, transfer it to the refrigerator a day before you plan to make pizza, so it can thaw slowly, and then let it sit at room temperature for 30 minutes before you roll it out.

Prepare a hot fire in a charcoal grill or preheat a gas grill on high. If the grill has a built-in thermometer, it should register between 500° and 600°F. Have ready a 14-inch, non-perforated pizza pan, preferably an inexpensive aluminum one.

While the grill is heating, place the onion, bell pepper, and garlic in a bowl. Toss the vegetables with the olive oil, oregano, red pepper flakes, and salt. Set aside.

Coat the pizza pan with vegetable-oil spray. Remove the dough from the plastic bag and place on a lightly floured work surface. Lightly dust the dough with flour. Using a rolling pin, roll the dough into a 10-inch round without rolling over the edges. Lift the dough occasionally to make sure it isn't sticking to the work surface. Shake the excess flour from the dough. Lay the dough on the prepared pizza pan and gently stretch it into a 14-inch round.

To top the pizza: Spread the marinara sauce over the crust, leaving a 1-inch border. Arrange the mixed vegetables evenly over the sauce. Scatter the artichokes over the top. Arrange the tomatoes in a single layer over the vegetables. Strew the olives over the top. Evenly distribute the cheese over the vegetables.

Place the pizza in the center of the grill directly over the hot fire and cover. (Work quickly so the grill temperature doesn't drop too much.) Grill the pizza until the crust is crisp and golden brown and the cheese is melted and bubbly, about 9 minutes.

Using a pizza peel or thick oven mitts, remove the pizza from the grill. Slice the pizza into wedges and serve immediately.

Grilled Tofu with Baby Bok Choy and Sweet Chile Sauce

Extra-firm tofu lightly charred on the grill holds its shape and turns wonderfully crisp on the outside and firm but creamy on the inside. The trick to grilling it successfully is to make sure it is well drained (lots of paper towels!) and generously brushed with oil before it goes on the grill. Once the tofu slices are over the fire, avoid lifting them or moving them around until it is time to turn them, so they stay intact. This dish is also good drizzled with Thai peanut sauce (see headnote, page 147).

[SERVES 4]

2 POUNDS EXTRA-FIRM TOFU, DRAINED

BABY BOK CHOY (PAGE 147)

VEGETABLE OIL

6 TABLESPOONS THAI SWEET CHILE SAUCE

Prepare a hot fire in a charcoal grill or preheat a gas grill on high.

Line a large, rimmed baking sheet with a double thickness of paper towels. Cut each cake of tofu into four $3/4$-inch-thick slices. Arrange the slices in a single layer on the paper towels. Place a double thickness of paper towels on top of the slices and press lightly to absorb the moisture. Prepare the bok choy while the grill heats.

When ready to grill, remove the paper towels and brush both sides of the tofu slices generously with vegetable oil. (Be careful when you turn the slices, or they may crack and crumble.) Oil the grill grate. Using a spatula, transfer the tofu slices to the grill, arranging them directly over the hot fire. Grill, turning once, until grill marks appear on both sides and the tofu is heated through, 2 to 3 minutes per side. If you have room on the grill grate, grill the bok choy while the tofu is grilling; otherwise, grill it as soon as the tofu comes off the grill, keeping the tofu warm.

To serve, arrange 3 bok choy halves in the center of each plate. Lay 2 tofu slices on top, overlapping them slightly. Drizzle about $1^{1}/_{2}$ tablespoons of the sweet chile sauce over the top and serve immediately.

Lemongrass-Grilled Tofu with Thai Peanut Sauce

When I'm grilling for my family, I have to split the grill space between the carnivores and the vegetarian! My husband, son, and I are the meat eaters (actually, anything eaters!), while my daughter, Molly, is a vegetarian. So, I try to get creative about how many ways I can grill tofu—and there are many. I have included two of Molly's favorite recipes in the book.

Lemongrass paste is quick to make, and easy enough for a weeknight, but if you have time on a weekend, make a big batch and store it in the freezer. It is good to have on hand because it is so versatile, delicious on beef, pork, shrimp, and, of course, tofu.

[SERVES 4]

2 POUNDS EXTRA-FIRM TOFU, DRAINED
½ CUP LEMONGRASS PASTE (PAGE 36)
VEGETABLE-OIL COOKING SPRAY
6 TABLESPOONS STORE-BOUGHT THAI PEANUT SAUCE
(SEE HEADNOTE, PAGE 147)

Prepare a hot fire in a charcoal grill or preheat a gas grill on high.

Line a large, rimmed baking sheet with a double thickness of paper towels. Cut each cake of tofu into four ¾-inch-thick slices. Arrange the slices in a single layer on the paper towels. Place a double thickness of paper towels on top and press lightly to absorb the moisture.

When ready to grill, remove the paper towels and brush both sides of the tofu slices generously with the lemongrass paste. (Be careful when you turn the slices, or they may crack and crumble.) Spray both sides of the tofu slices with vegetable-oil spray to prevent the tofu from sticking to the grill.

Oil the grill grate. Using a spatula, transfer the tofu slices to the grill, arranging them directly over the hot fire. Grill, turning once, until grill marks appear on both sides and the tofu is heated through, 2 to 3 minutes per side.

To serve, arrange 2 tofu slices, overlapping them slightly, in the center of each plate. Drizzle about 1½ tablespoons of the peanut sauce over the top of each plate and serve immediately.

Portabella Mushroom Burger
with Grilled Onions and Pesto Mayonnaise

Here's a recipe with room for improvisation! Grilled portabella mushrooms make tasty burgers, whether you dress them up with pesto mayonnaise, plain mayonnaise, steak sauce, or traditional ketchup and relish. I love to eat them with grilled onions and lots of lettuce. If you have time, cut a sweet red bell pepper into quarters, brush it with olive oil, and grill it along with the onion, for a dynamite stack of smoky grilled vegetables tucked in a bun.

[SERVES 4]

1 TABLESPOON STORE-BOUGHT BASIL PESTO	FRESHLY GROUND PEPPER
¼ CUP MAYONNAISE	1 TABLESPOON BALSAMIC VINEGAR
4 PORTABELLA MUSHROOMS	4 SESAME-SEED HAMBURGER BUNS,
1 WALLA WALLA OR OTHER SWEET ONION,	SPLIT
CUT INTO FOUR ½-INCH-THICK SLICES	4 LETTUCE LEAVES
EXTRA-VIRGIN OLIVE OIL	4 RIPE TOMATO SLICES (OPTIONAL)
KOSHER OR SEA SALT	

Prepare a hot fire in a charcoal grill or preheat a gas grill on high.

In a small bowl, stir together the pesto and mayonnaise, mixing well. Set aside.

Stem the mushrooms and wipe the caps clean with a damp paper towel. If desired, use a spoon to scoop away the dark brown gills from the underside of each cap. (I think the mushrooms taste meatier when the gills are left intact.) Arrange the mushrooms and onion slices in a single layer on a large, rimmed baking sheet and brush them on both sides with olive oil. Sprinkle with salt and pepper. Brush the gill side of the mushrooms with balsamic vinegar.

Oil the grill grate. Arrange the onions and the mushrooms, smooth side down, directly over the hot fire and grill until grill marks appear, about 4 minutes for the onions and 3 minutes for the mushrooms. Turn the onions and mushrooms and grill the mushrooms until tender, about 3 minutes longer, and the onions until seared with grill marks, about 4 minutes longer. (Use a combination of tongs and a long-handled spatula to turn the onion slices so they stay intact.) If there is room, place the buns, cut side down, on the grill to toast during the last minute the vegetables are cooking. Or, put the buns on the grill to toast when you remove the mushrooms, which should be ready before the onions.

To serve, smear the bottom half of each bun with some of the pesto mayonnaise. Top with a mushroom, an onion slice, a lettuce leaf, and a tomato slice, if desired. Serve immediately.

TREASURED SIDES

WHEN I WAS DEVELOPING THE CHAPTERS for this book, I thought, "How can I offer so many recipes for grilled meats, poultry, and fish without suggesting side dishes to accompany them?" A perfectly grilled steak on a plate is a joy, but you need something sitting alongside it to complete the meal. This chapter is filled with some of my favorite side dishes. Since not all of my favorites would fit, I call these my treasured sides. The criteria for inclusion were, of course, being delicious and drawing on flavors from around the globe, but also being relatively quick to make.

Grilled polenta, smothered with grilled sweet onions and red bell peppers and then showered with Parmesan, is my idea of a perfect side. When I'm in a hurry, I buy the ready-made polenta in a tube and cut it into thick slices. When not so rushed, I make my own, and I've included an easy recipe (page 168). Polenta works well with grilled chicken, and though it is Italian, it pairs well with French-inspired Mustard-and-Rosemary-Crusted Lamb Steaks (page 57), too.

Couscous is a constant pantry staple for me. In the time it takes to boil water, I can have ingredients chopped and ready to add, and within ten minutes the couscous is ready to eat. I regularly vary the seasonings and ingredients, substituting currants for the dried cranberries, or adding slivered green onions or chopped red onions.

I always keep orzo, bulgur, and fun-shaped dried pastas in the pantry, as well. These quick-cooking grains and pastas make it easy to efficiently cook an entire week-night meal. The same is true for canned beans, such as black beans and chickpeas. A well-stocked pantry usually means I can put together a simple black bean salad, or combine chickpeas with cherry tomatoes, feta, olives, and herbs for a healthy side, without needing to make a trip to the grocery store.

Grilled Polenta with Sweet Red Peppers and Onion Wedges

It wasn't until I started writing this book that I tried precooked polenta sold in tubes. Even though I'd noticed it in the refrigerated case at the grocery store, along with all the packages of fresh pasta, I always thought, "Why bother when it's so easy to make from scratch?" For quick weeknight meals and fast grilling, though, it's a great product: It takes less than five minutes to slip it out of the package, slice it, and brush it with olive oil. To dress it up, I grill sweet red peppers and onions and top with some grated Parmesan.

[SERVES 5]

1   TUBE (18 OUNCES) PRECOOKED POLENTA, SUCH
    AS SAN GENNARO BRAND (SEE COOK'S NOTE)
EXTRA-VIRGIN OLIVE OIL
KOSHER OR SEA SALT
FRESHLY GROUND PEPPER

2   RED BELL PEPPERS, QUARTERED LENGTH-
    WISE, SEEDED, AND DERIBBED
1   LARGE WALLA WALLA OR OTHER SWEET
    ONION, CUT INTO ½-INCH-THICK SLICES
¼   CUP FRESHLY GRATED PARMIGIANO-
    REGGIANO CHEESE

Prepare a hot fire in a charcoal grill or preheat a gas grill on high.

Trim off the irregular ends and slice the polenta into ten ½-inch-thick slices. Arrange on a rimmed baking sheet. Generously brush the slices on both sides with olive oil and season lightly with salt and pepper. Brush the peppers and onions with olive oil, coating them lightly.

Oil the grill grate. Arrange the polenta slices directly over the hot fire and grill, turning once, until they have grill marks etched across both sides, 8 to 10 minutes total. While the polenta is grilling, arrange the peppers and onions directly over the hot fire and grill, turning once, until the edges begin to char and the peppers and onions are tender but still firm, about 5 minutes total. (Use tongs and a spatula to turn the onion slices.)

To serve, cut the peppers into thin strips, and slice the onion rounds in half. Arrange 2 polenta slices, slightly overlapping them, on each plate and top with some peppers and onions. Sprinkle with the cheese and serve immediately.

COOK'S NOTE If you prefer to make your own polenta, here's a quick and easy cooking method: Combine 1½ cups polenta, ½ teaspoon kosher or sea salt, and 6 cups water or canned low-sodium chicken broth in a large, microwave-safe bowl. Cover and microwave on high for 10 minutes. Stir well, cover, and continue to microwave on high for another 5 minutes. Spread the hot polenta evenly on a buttered large, rimmed baking sheet, forming a rectangle ½ inch thick. Let cool, cover, and refrigerate until set, about 1 hour. Cut into squares and grill.

Lemon Couscous with Dried Cranberries and Apricots

Perfect with grilled foods, especially lamb, pork, and poultry, or even Eggplant with *Herbes de Provence* (page 148) for a nonmeat combination. Couscous is a snap to make on the stove top, but the microwave is another quick-cooking option, plus it saves cleaning a pot: Place the couscous and dried fruits in a heatproof 3-quart serving bowl, bring the broth to a boil in the microwave, pour the broth over the couscous, add the olive oil and seasonings, and stir to combine. Cover with plastic wrap and set aside. Fluff, and then add the toasted nuts and green onions just before serving.

2	CUPS CANNED LOW-SODIUM CHICKEN BROTH
3	TABLESPOONS MEYER LEMON–FLAVORED EXTRA-VIRGIN OLIVE OIL (SEE COOK'S NOTE, PAGE 106)
½	TEASPOON KOSHER OR SEA SALT
½	TEASPOON FRESHLY GROUND PEPPER
1½	CUPS OR 1 BOX (10 OUNCES) QUICK-COOKING COUSCOUS (SEE COOK'S NOTE)
⅓	CUP DRIED CRANBERRIES
⅓	CUP DICED DRIED APRICOTS
⅓	CUP PINE NUTS
2	GREEN ONIONS, INCLUDING GREEN TOPS, THINLY SLICED

[SERVES 6]

In a 3-quart saucepan, bring the broth to a boil. Add the olive oil, salt, and pepper. Stir in the couscous, cranberries, and apricots, cover, and remove from the heat. Let stand for 5 to 10 minutes.

In the meantime, heat a small, dry heavy skillet over medium-high heat. When hot but not smoking, add the pine nuts and toast them, stirring constantly, until lightly browned, about 3 minutes. Transfer to a small plate.

When ready to serve, fluff the couscous with a fork, and stir in the pine nuts and green onions. Transfer to a warmed serving bowl and serve immediately.

 COOK'S NOTE Boxes of flavored couscous fill market shelves. For this recipe, you need to look for unseasoned (plain) couscous, usually sold in 10-ounce boxes. If you cannot find unseasoned couscous, just buy any box and discard the seasoning packet inside. Alternatively, buy couscous sold in bulk.

Israeli Couscous with Zucchini, Red Bell Pepper, and Parsley

For this recipe, you need to look for Casbah brand original toasted couscous, giant pasta pearls, or a similarly labeled product. Although these large semolina beads are commonly known as Israeli couscous, that term does not appear on the box. With the addition of some colorful vegetables and herbs, this nutty Mediterranean pasta makes a wonderful accompaniment to grilled meats, fish, and poultry. It can be served hot or at room temperature, making it an ideal no-fuss side dish for family meals or entertaining.

[SERVES 4 TO 6]

2	TABLESPOONS EXTRA-VIRGIN OLIVE OIL
1	SMALL YELLOW ONION, DICED
1	TEASPOON MINCED GARLIC
1¼	CUPS TOASTED (ISRAELI) COUSCOUS
2	CUPS CANNED LOW-SODIUM CHICKEN BROTH
½	TEASPOON FRESHLY GROUND PEPPER
1	ZUCCHINI, ENDS TRIMMED, CUT INTO ¼-INCH DICE
1	SMALL RED BELL PEPPER, SEEDED, DERIBBED, AND CUT INTO ¼-INCH DICE
2	TABLESPOONS MINCED FRESH FLAT-LEAF PARSLEY

In a sauté pan with a tight-fitting lid, heat the olive oil over medium heat. Swirl to coat the pan, add the onion and garlic, and sauté, stirring constantly, until just beginning to soften, about 2 minutes. Add the couscous and stir constantly until lightly browned, 2 to 3 minutes. Add the chicken broth and pepper and bring to a simmer. Turn the heat to low, cover, and simmer until almost all of the liquid is absorbed, about 8 minutes.

Stir in the zucchini and bell pepper, cover, and cook until the zucchini is bright green and tender, 3 minutes longer. Stir in the parsley, transfer to a warmed serving bowl, and serve immediately.

Orzo Salad with Kalamata Olives, Red and Yellow Bell Peppers, and Feta

Here's a do-ahead salad perfect with grilled meats, poultry, and some fish dishes. It's a fabulous accompaniment to grilled lamb, especially Rosemary-and-Garlic-Crusted Lamb Chops (page 60) or Lamb Steaks with *Herbes de Provence* Spice Rub (page 56). Or, serve this salad alongside Lemon-and-Oregano-Grilled Halibut Skewers (page 93) or Chicken Breasts with Tarragon-Mustard Paste (page 112).

	1	TEASPOON KOSHER OR SEA SALT
	2	CUPS (ABOUT 12 OUNCES) ORZO (RICE-SHAPED PASTA)
	2	TABLESPOONS EXTRA-VIRGIN OLIVE OIL
	1	LARGE RED BELL PEPPER, SEEDED, DERIBBED, AND CUT INTO ½-INCH DICE
[SERVES 6 TO 8]	1	LARGE YELLOW OR ORANGE BELL PEPPER, SEEDED, DERIBBED, AND CUT INTO ½-INCH DICE
	6	OUNCES FETA CHEESE, CRUMBLED
	1	CUP PITTED AND HALVED KALAMATA OLIVES
	4	GREEN ONIONS, INCLUDING GREEN TOPS, THINLY SLICED
	6	TABLESPOONS EXTRA-VIRGIN OLIVE OIL
	2½	TABLESPOONS FRESH LEMON JUICE
DRESSING	2	CLOVES GARLIC, MINCED
	¼	CUP CHOPPED FRESH FLAT-LEAF PARSLEY
	¾	TEASPOON KOSHER OR SEA SALT
	1	TEASPOON FRESHLY GROUND PEPPER

Fill a 4-quart saucepan two-thirds full of water and bring to a boil over high heat. Add 1 teaspoon salt to the boiling water, then add the orzo. Stir and cook the pasta until al dente (cooked through but still slightly chewy), 8 to 10 minutes. Drain the pasta, rinse with cold water, and drain thoroughly again. Transfer the orzo to a large bowl and toss with the olive oil. Add the bell peppers, cheese, olives, and green onions.

To make the dressing, in a small bowl, whisk together the olive oil, lemon juice, garlic, parsley, salt, and pepper. Taste and adjust the seasoning.

Add the dressing to the salad and toss gently to combine. Serve immediately, or cover and refrigerate until ready to serve. Refrigerate for up to 2 days. Remove from the refrigerator 30 minutes before serving.

Grilled Sweet Corn, Black Bean, and Cherry Tomato Salad

In summer, I like to do as much cooking on the grill as possible. That means my side dishes are either made ahead or are something I can grill along with my main course. This salad has elements of both. When I know I am going to make it, I grill extra corn on the previous night so I have leftovers. Also, rather than turn on the oven or fuss with a skillet, you can cook the bacon in the microwave: Slip the bacon slices between a pair of paper towels and microwave on high for 3 to 4 minutes until crisp. Once the bacon cools slightly, you can crumble it. Saving time with the corn and bacon makes this salad a breeze to make. It's perfect with grilled meats and poultry, especially recipes with Southwest flavors, such as Hanger Steaks with Chile-Rubbed Grilled Onions (page 50) and Southwest Chipotle Chile–Grilled Chicken Breasts (page 111).

	½	CUP EXTRA-VIRGIN OLIVE OIL
	2	TABLESPOONS CIDER VINEGAR
	2	TEASPOONS WHOLE-GRAIN MUSTARD
DRESSING	¾	TEASPOON ADOBO SAUCE FROM CANNED CHIPOTLE CHILES
	1	TEASPOON KOSHER OR SEA SALT
	1	TEASPOON SUGAR
	½	TEASPOON FRESHLY GROUND PEPPER
	2	EARS SWEET CORN IN THE HUSK (PAGE 141)
	1	CAN (15 OUNCES) BLACK BEANS, RINSED AND DRAINED
	12	CHERRY TOMATOES, QUARTERED
[SERVES 4]	5	SLICES COOKED BACON, CRUMBLED
	2	GREEN ONIONS, INCLUDING GREEN TOPS, CUT ON THE DIAGONAL INTO ¼-INCH-THICK SLICES
	¼	CUP COARSELY CHOPPED FRESH CILANTRO

To make the dressing, in a small bowl, whisk together the olive oil, vinegar, mustard, adobo sauce, salt, sugar, and pepper. Set aside.

If the husks are still attached to the ears of corn, remove and discard them. Working with one ear at a time, stand it upright, stem end down, in a large bowl. Using a sharp knife, cut downward along the cob, removing the kernels and rotating the cob a quarter turn after each cut. Discard the cobs.

Add the black beans, tomatoes, bacon, green onions, and cilantro to the corn in the bowl. Add the dressing and toss gently to coat all the ingredients evenly. Serve immediately, or cover and set aside until ready to serve.

Bulgur Salad with Smoky Grilled Tomatoes and Green Onions

This twist on the traditional Middle Eastern grain salad known as tabbouleh is simple to assemble and delightfully refreshing. It is a natural accompaniment to grilled meats, poultry, and fish. I call for Smoky Grill-Roasted Roma Tomatoes with Garlic (page 153) in the recipe, which brings a big tomato and garlic flavor to the salad. Plan ahead and grill the tomatoes so you have them on hand. Otherwise, chop 3 fresh Roma tomatoes and use 2 teaspoons minced garlic in the dressing.

[SERVES 4 TO 6]

1	CUP MEDIUM-GRIND BULGUR (SEE COOK'S NOTE)
2	CUPS BOILING WATER
2	GREEN ONIONS, INCLUDING GREEN TOPS, THINLY SLICED
3	SMOKY GRILL-ROASTED ROMA TOMATOES WITH GARLIC (PAGE 153), CHOPPED
½	CUP CHOPPED FRESH FLAT-LEAF PARSLEY

DRESSING

3	TABLESPOONS EXTRA-VIRGIN OLIVE OIL
1½	TEASPOONS BALSAMIC VINEGAR
1	TEASPOON MINCED GARLIC
½	TEASPOON KOSHER OR SEA SALT
½	TEASPOON FRESHLY GROUND PEPPER
½	TEASPOON SUGAR
⅛	TEASPOON CAYENNE PEPPER

Place the bulgur in a large heatproof bowl, add the boiling water, and let stand until softened, 30 to 40 minutes. Drain the bulgur in a large sieve, pressing out as much water as possible. Dry the bowl and return the bulgur to the bowl. Add the green onions, tomatoes and their juices, and parsley.

To make the dressing, in a small bowl, whisk together the olive oil, vinegar, garlic, salt, pepper, sugar, and cayenne pepper. Taste and adjust the seasoning.

Add the dressing to the salad and toss gently to combine. Serve immediately, or cover and refrigerate until ready to serve.

 COOK'S NOTE Bulgur comes in three grinds: fine, medium, and coarse. When the grain is sold in bulk at natural-foods stores, the bins are usually labeled according to the grind. If you are buying bulgur in a box, check the label to make sure you are purchasing medium grind.

Asian Noodle Salad with Cilantro and Black Sesame Seeds

Grilled fish, especially salmon, pairs well with this Asian noodle salad. Look for black sesame seeds in the bulk-foods section of natural-foods stores or Asian markets. Store sesame seeds in the freezer to keep them from turning rancid.

[SERVES 4]

3	PACKAGES (2 OUNCES EACH) BEAN THREAD NOODLES (SEE COOK'S NOTE)
¼	CUP SOY SAUCE
1	TABLESPOON RICE VINEGAR
3	TABLESPOONS ASIAN SESAME OIL
2	TEASPOONS SUGAR
2	TEASPOONS PEELED AND MINCED FRESH GINGER
1	LARGE CARROT, PEELED AND JULIENNED
1	LARGE STALK CELERY, JULIENNED
2	GREEN ONIONS, INCLUDING GREEN TOPS, CUT INTO MATCHSTICKS
½	CUP PACKED FRESH CILANTRO LEAVES
2	TABLESPOONS BLACK SESAME SEEDS

In a large bowl, soak the bean thread noodles in hot water to cover until softened, about 20 minutes. Drain well in a colander, shaking the colander a few times to make sure all the water is removed. Pat the noodles dry with paper towels.

To make the salad, in a large bowl, whisk together the soy sauce, vinegar, sesame oil, sugar, and ginger. Add the noodles and toss until well coated with the dressing. Add the carrot, celery, green onions, cilantro, and sesame seeds and toss to distribute all the ingredients evenly.

Serve immediately, or cover and refrigerate until ready to serve or for up to 2 days. Remove from the refrigerator 30 minutes before serving.

COOK'S NOTE Bean thread noodles, also known as Chinese vermicelli or cellophane noodles, are translucent noodles made from mung bean starch. Once softened, they have a wonderfully chewy, yet tender texture. Bean thread noodles typically come in 2-ounce cellophane packages, usually bundled in groups of 6 or 8 and wrapped in neon pink or clear plastic mesh bags. Look for them in well-stocked supermarkets and Asian grocery stores.

Grilled Fig and Green Bean Salad with Walnut Vinaigrette

This salad is a work of art on the plate: Crisp-tender green beans mingle with voluptuous grilled figs and toasted walnuts slicked with nut oil. Crumbles of creamy-white goat cheese spill over the field of garden hues—brilliant green, blue-black, and burnished brown—to create one of the best salads I know. Make this recipe when fresh figs are in the market, usually late summer and early fall. Grill extra figs and serve them for dessert the following night, drizzled with honey and accompanied with slices of Manchego cheese, a sheep's-milk cheese from Spain's La Mancha region.

	⅓	CUP WALNUT OIL (SEE COOK'S NOTE)
	2	TABLESPOONS RICE VINEGAR
VINAIGRETTE	1	TABLESPOON MINCED SHALLOT
	1	TEASPOON SUGAR
	½	TEASPOON KOSHER OR SEA SALT
		FRESHLY GROUND PEPPER
	1	TABLESPOON PLUS ¼ TEASPOON KOSHER OR SEA SALT
	1	POUND YOUNG, TENDER GREEN BEANS, STEM ENDS TRIMMED
	½	CUP CHOPPED WALNUTS
[SERVES 6]	2	TEASPOONS WALNUT OIL
	12	RIPE BLACK MISSION FIGS, HALVED LENGTHWISE
		EXTRA-VIRGIN OLIVE OIL
	3	OUNCES FRESH GOAT CHEESE

To make the vinaigrette, in a small bowl, whisk together the walnut oil, vinegar, shallot, sugar, salt, and pepper to taste. Set aside.

Fill a large stockpot two-thirds full of water, cover, and bring to a boil. Have ready a large bowl of ice water. Add 1 tablespoon of the salt to the boiling water, then the beans, and cook until bright green and crisp-tender, 2 to 4 minutes. Drain the beans and plunge them into the ice water until cold, 1 to 2 minutes. Drain, wrap in several layers of paper towels, and place in a plastic bag. Refrigerate until 30 minutes before serving.

 COOK'S NOTE Walnut oil adds an unctuous, nutty-rich flavor to salads. As with all nut oils, always refrigerate walnut oil after opening so it does not become rancid.

Meanwhile, preheat the oven to 325°F. In a bowl, toss the walnuts with the remaining $1/4$ teaspoon salt and the walnut oil. Spread the nuts on a rimmed baking sheet and toast in the oven until fragrant and lightly browned, 8 to 10 minutes. Set aside.

Prepare a medium fire in a charcoal grill or preheat a gas grill on medium. Brush the figs on all sides with olive oil.

Oil the grill grate, or arrange the figs cut side down on an oiled grill grid or basket (see page 26). Grill the figs directly over the medium fire just until grill marks appear, about 1 minute. Turn and grill until tender but still firm when pierced with a knife, about 1 minute longer. Transfer to a plate and set aside to cool for 10 minutes.

In a large bowl, combine the beans and figs and toss gently with the vinaigrette. Divide among salad plates. Garnish with the walnuts and crumble the goat cheese on top. Serve immediately.

Bruschetta

Here's an easy and versatile accompaniment to almost any main course, especially a grilled main course. Instead of warming bread in the oven to serve with dinner, I grill slices to make bruschetta and serve it with prepared toppings, such as tapenade, herbed goat cheese, fennel relish, or sweet red pepper spread. Of course, the traditional topping of diced tomatoes with a bit of minced garlic and torn leaves of fresh basil is terrific, too. For casual entertaining, make bruschetta the starter, grilling it first, then grill the main course while everyone is sipping drinks, mingling, and munching on this warm Italian appetizer.

1	1-POUND LOAF COUNTRY-STYLE BREAD OR LARGE, CRUSTY BAGUETTE
[SERVES 8]	EXTRA-VIRGIN OLIVE OIL
2	CLOVES GARLIC, HALVED

Prepare a hot fire in a charcoal grill or preheat a gas grill on high.

Cut the bread crosswise into slices about 1 inch thick. Arrange the slices in a single layer on a large, rimmed baking sheet and generously brush the slices on both sides with olive oil.

Arrange the slices on the grill grate directly over the hot fire, and grill, turning once, until they have attractive grill marks on both sides and are golden brown at the edges, 4 to 5 minutes total.

Remove from the grill and rub each slice with the cut side of the garlic. Drizzle with a little more olive oil, if desired.

Carrot Salad with Cumin and Mint

Packaged shredded carrots streamline the assembly of this salad. It is a colorful and healthy side dish to a grilled main course, especially if you also serve some grilled zucchini or asparagus and skip a starch altogether. This salad is a favorite of mine when I am grilling lamb, and it would complement any of the grilled lamb recipes in Chapter 3.

	⅓ CUP EXTRA-VIRGIN OLIVE OIL
	4 TEASPOONS FRESH LEMON JUICE
	1 TABLESPOON HONEY
DRESSING	2 TEASPOONS GROUND CUMIN
	¾ TEASPOON KOSHER OR SEA SALT
	⅛ TEASPOON CAYENNE PEPPER
	FRESHLY GROUND PEPPER
	1 PACKAGE (10 OUNCES) SHREDDED CARROTS
[SERVES 6]	1 FENNEL BULB, HALVED LENGTHWISE, CORED, AND THINLY SLICED LENGTHWISE
	½ CUP COARSELY CHOPPED FRESH MINT

To make the dressing, in a small bowl, whisk together the olive oil, lemon juice, honey, cumin, salt, cayenne pepper, and pepper to taste.

In a bowl, combine the carrots, fennel, and mint. Add the dressing and toss gently to coat all the ingredients evenly. Serve immediately, or cover and refrigerate until ready to serve or for up to 8 hours. Remove from the refrigerator 30 minutes before serving.

Middle Eastern Chickpea Salad

This bright-tasting chickpea salad is a twist on a traditional Lebanese vegetable salad. It has big flavors and takes little effort to prepare, which is what I am looking for on weeknights. The salad can be served right away, but is at its best when the chickpeas are allowed to absorb some of the dressing and all the flavors meld. Serve it with grilled chicken, pork, halibut, swordfish, or shrimp.

DRESSING

6	TABLESPOONS EXTRA-VIRGIN OLIVE OIL
	FRESHLY GRATED ZEST OF 1 LEMON
2	TABLESPOONS FRESH LEMON JUICE
1	LARGE CLOVE GARLIC, MINCED
1	TEASPOON KOSHER OR SEA SALT
½	TEASPOON FRESHLY GROUND PEPPER
⅛	TEASPOON CAYENNE PEPPER

[SERVES 6]

2	CANS (15.5 OUNCES EACH) CHICKPEAS, RINSED AND DRAINED
1	CAN (6 OUNCES DRAINED WEIGHT) PITTED RIPE OLIVES, HALVED
1	PINT CHERRY TOMATOES, HALVED
1	CUP LOOSELY PACKED FRESH FLAT-LEAF PARSLEY LEAVES
4	OUNCES FETA CHEESE, CRUMBLED

To make the dressing, in a small bowl, whisk together the olive oil, lemon zest, lemon juice, garlic, salt, pepper, and cayenne pepper.

In a large bowl, combine the chickpeas, olives, tomatoes, parsley, and feta. Add the dressing and toss gently to combine. Set aside at room temperature for 30 minutes to allow the flavors to develop. Alternatively, cover and refrigerate until ready to serve or for up to 2 days. Remove from the refrigerator 30 minutes before serving.

Grilled Fingerling Potatoes
with Crumbled Blue Cheese Sauce

While traveling and ruminating on recipe ideas for this book, I met a friend for a drink and we enjoyed an appetizer of Idaho potato skins with a blue cheese dipping sauce. It made me think about how good a blue cheese sauce can be, especially one packed with fat crumbles of blue cheese and served with grilled fingerling potatoes. Here's the recipe, which is perfect with grilled steak.

		1 TO 1¼ POUNDS FINGERLING POTATOES
[SERVES 4]	2	TABLESPOONS EXTRA-VIRGIN OLIVE OIL
		KOSHER OR SEA SALT
		FRESHLY GROUND PEPPER
	½	CUP PLAIN LOW-FAT YOGURT OR SOUR CREAM
	½	CUP MAYONNAISE
BLUE	2	TEASPOONS DIJON MUSTARD
CHEESE	1	TABLESPOON SUGAR
SAUCE	½	TEASPOON FRESHLY GROUND PEPPER
	3	TABLESPOONS MINCED FRESH FLAT-LEAF PARSLEY
	2	TABLESPOONS SNIPPED FRESH CHIVES
	3	OUNCES BLUE CHEESE, CRUMBLED (SEE COOK'S NOTE)

Prepare a medium-hot fire in a charcoal grill or preheat a gas grill on medium-high.

Poke the potatoes in several places with the tines of a fork. Place the potatoes in a bowl and toss with the olive oil. Season with salt and pepper.

To create a cool zone, bank the coals to one side of the grill or turn off one of the burners. Oil the grill grate. Arrange the potatoes in a single layer on the cool side of the grill, cover, and grill until they are tender when pierced with a knife, 18 to 20 minutes.

While the potatoes are grilling, make the sauce: In a bowl, whisk together the yogurt, mayonnaise, mustard, sugar, and pepper. Using a rubber spatula, gently mix in the parsley, chives, and cheese. Serve immediately, or cover and refrigerate for up to 3 days. Remove from the refrigerator 30 minutes before serving.

Serve the potatoes piping hot with the sauce drizzled over the top or served on the side.

 COOK'S NOTE A number of wonderful blue cheeses are being made in the United States nowadays. I am especially fond of tangy, rich blues, such as Point Reyes blue from California, Rogue Creamery blue from Oregon, and Maytag blue from Iowa.

THE GRILL PLANNER—SECOND HELPINGS

I COULDN'T RESIST WRITING THIS CHAPTER.

I consider myself the queen of leftovers, so offering a whole chapter of recipes that utilize grilled leftovers was irresistible. Just think, firing up the grill once and cooking extra means another night's dinner is almost at hand. A couple of extra sweet peppers and onions on the grill, which adds no more grilling time, puts you steps ahead when you make Penne Pasta with Grilled Sweet Peppers, Grilled Onions, and Basil (page 196) the next night. Or, cooking one or two extra tuna fillets translates to Pepper-Crusted Ahi Tuna Salad Niçoise (page 187), a hearty main-course salad, later in the week. This is how I think and plan, and this is how I successfully manage weeknight meals. I hope this chapter inspires you to do the same.

Grilled Asparagus Salad with Soft Poached Egg, Prosciutto, and Lemon-Parmesan Vinaigrette

One Sunday morning, while rummaging around in the refrigerator for something to serve my family for brunch, I came up with this idea. I had on hand leftover grilled asparagus, slices of prosciutto, and eggs. It seemed like a good idea to lay slices of prosciutto on a warmed plate, arrange spears of asparagus over the top, and then set a couple of poached eggs on the asparagus. It needed a sauce to pull it together, so I made a lemon vinaigrette and added fresh tarragon from my herb pot. Tarragon and eggs are perfect partners, and all the elements came together deliciously. Serve for brunch or as a light supper with crusty rolls.

	6	TABLESPOONS EXTRA-VIRGIN OLIVE OIL
	2½	TABLESPOONS FRESH LEMON JUICE
LEMON-	2	TABLESPOONS MINCED FRESH TARRAGON
PARMESAN	1½	TABLESPOONS FRESHLY GRATED PARMIGIANO-REGGIANO CHEESE
VINAIGRETTE	1	TEASPOON MINCED GARLIC
	½	TEASPOON KOSHER OR SEA SALT
	½	TEASPOON FRESHLY GROUND PEPPER
	2	TEASPOONS WHITE VINEGAR
	1	TEASPOON KOSHER OR SEA SALT
[SERVES 4]	8	LARGE EGGS, EACH CRACKED INTO A SMALL RAMEKIN OR CUSTARD CUP
	8	PAPER-THIN SLICES PROSCIUTTO
	28	GRILLED ASPARAGUS SPEARS (PAGE 140)

To make the vinaigrette, in a small jar with a tight-fitting lid, combine the olive oil, lemon juice, tarragon, cheese, garlic, salt, and pepper. Cover tightly and shake vigorously to blend. Taste and adjust the seasoning. Set aside.

Bring water to a depth of 2 inches to a boil in a large skillet or sauté pan. Add the vinegar and salt and lower the heat so the water barely simmers. One by one, slip each egg into the water, evenly spacing them apart. Cook the eggs until the whites are set and the yolks have filmed over but are still runny, 3 to 4 minutes. Remove with a slotted spoon to a plate lined with a double thickness of paper towels to blot the excess water.

While the water is coming to a boil and the eggs are cooking, arrange 2 prosciutto slices in the center of each warmed dinner plate. Arrange 7 asparagus spears on top. Using the slotted spoon, transfer 2 poached eggs to each plate, placing them in the center over the asparagus. Give the vinaigrette a last-minute shake and drizzle about 2 tablespoons over each salad. Serve immediately.

Pepper-Crusted Ahi Tuna Salad Niçoise

A traditional *salade niçoise* calls for canned tuna, but I think this classic of southern France never tastes as good as it does when made with grilled fresh tuna. When it comes to main-course salads, I'm a bit of a grazer. I like varied and interesting bites, and this salad provides that. One moment I have a succulent piece of tuna in my mouth, the next a bite of creamy potato infused with a mustardy vinaigrette, and the next a nibble of rich Niçoise olive. Serve with a crusty baguette to complete the meal.

	½	CUP EXTRA-VIRGIN OLIVE OIL
	3	TABLESPOONS FRESH LEMON JUICE
	2	TEASPOONS DIJON MUSTARD
VINAIGRETTE	1	TEASPOON FINELY MINCED OIL-PACKED ANCHOVIES
	½	TEASPOON KOSHER OR SEA SALT
	½	TEASPOON SUGAR
	½	TEASPOON FRESHLY GROUND PEPPER

	12	OUNCES NEW RED POTATOES
	2	TEASPOONS KOSHER OR SEA SALT
	12	OUNCES TENDER, YOUNG GREEN BEANS OR HARICOTS VERTS, STEM ENDS TRIMMED
	8	WHOLE ROMAINE LEAVES, ENDS TRIMMED
[SERVES 4]	2	HARD-COOKED EGGS, EACH CUT INTO 6 WEDGES (SEE COOK'S NOTE, PAGE 188)
	2	LARGE, RIPE TOMATOES, EACH CUT INTO 8 WEDGES
	2	PEPPER-CRUSTED AHI TUNA STEAKS (PAGE 97), CUT INTO ¼-INCH-THICK SLICES
	⅓	CUP NIÇOISE OLIVES, DRAINED
	⅓	CUP MINCED FRESH FLAT-LEAF PARSLEY

To make the vinaigrette, in a small jar with a tight-fitting lid, combine the olive oil, lemon juice, mustard, anchovies, ½ teaspoon salt, the sugar, and pepper. Cover tightly and shake vigorously to blend. Taste and adjust the seasoning. Set aside.

Scrub the potatoes but leave the skins on. In a saucepan, combine the potatoes with water to cover by 1 inch. Add 1 teaspoon of the salt and bring to a boil. Adjust the heat so the water just simmers, cover partially, and cook the potatoes until tender when pierced with a fork, about 20 minutes. Drain, let cool slightly, and cut into quarters. »

Pepper-Crusted Ahi Tuna Salad Niçoise
(continued)

While the potatoes are cooking, fill a saucepan two-thirds full of water and bring to a boil. Have a bowl of ice water ready. Add the remaining 1 teaspoon salt and the green beans to the boiling water and cook the beans just until bright green and crisp-tender, about 4 minutes. (If using haricots verts, cook for only 2 to 3 minutes.) Use tongs or a sieve to transfer the beans to the ice water. Once cold, drain the beans and blot dry with paper towels.

To assemble the salad, place 2 romaine leaves, slightly overlapping, on each of 4 dinner plates, or arrange all 8 leaves on 1 large round or rectangular platter. Arrange the potatoes, beans, eggs, tomatoes, and tuna slices in rows or piles, placing each ingredient side by side on top of the romaine. (I like to arrange the beans between the potatoes and eggs for maximum color contrast.) Divide and scatter the olives and parsley over the top. Give the vinaigrette a last-minute shake and drizzle over the salad. Serve immediately.

 COOK'S NOTE Here's how to hard-cook an egg so that no green coats the yolk: Place the eggs in a small saucepan. Add cold water to cover by 1 inch, and a pinch of salt. Bring to a boil, and then immediately reduce the temperature to low; the water should barely simmer. Set a timer for 11 minutes. As soon as the timer goes off, pour off the boiling water and run cold water over the eggs until they are cool enough to handle. Peel under running water. If you're not using the eggs immediately, leave the shells on and refrigerate for up to five days. Write "HB" on the shells with a pencil to remind you the eggs have been cooked.

Composed Salad of Alder-Planked Salmon and Asparagus with Lemon Vinaigrette

This main-course salad is a classic example of advance planning. Grill extra salmon and asparagus on a previous night, and all you need to do at dinnertime is make the vinaigrette, toast the pine nuts, warm the salmon and asparagus enough to take the chill off, and "compose" the salads. Add a crusty baguette and you have a light, simple meal for dining alfresco on a warm summer night.

LEMON VINAIGRETTE

¼ CUP EXTRA-VIRGIN OLIVE OIL
1 TEASPOON FRESHLY GRATED LEMON ZEST
2 TABLESPOONS FRESH LEMON JUICE
1 CLOVE GARLIC, MINCED
½ TEASPOON DIJON MUSTARD
½ TEASPOON SUGAR
¾ TEASPOON KOSHER OR SEA SALT
FRESHLY GROUND PEPPER

[SERVES 4]

½ CUP PINE NUTS
28 GRILLED ASPARAGUS SPEARS (PAGE 140), WARMED
4 PORTIONS ALDER-PLANKED SALMON WITH LEMON-VODKA-DILL MARINADE (PAGE 84), WARMED
¼ CUP 1-INCH-LONG FRESH CHIVES

To make the lemon vinaigrette, in a small jar with a tight-fitting lid, combine the olive oil, lemon zest and juice, garlic, mustard, sugar, salt, and lots of pepper. (Several good grinds of pepper make the vinaigrette taste robust.) Cover tightly and shake vigorously to blend. Taste and adjust the seasoning. Set aside.

Heat a small, dry heavy skillet over medium-high heat. When hot but not smoking, add the pine nuts and toast them, stirring constantly, until lightly browned, about 3 minutes. Transfer to a small plate.

To arrange the salad, fan 7 spears of asparagus on each dinner plate. Place a salmon fillet in the center of each plate, on top of the asparagus. Scatter the pine nuts over the plates. Give the vinaigrette a last-minute shake and drizzle an equal amount over each salad. Garnish with the chives and serve immediately.

Grilled Sweet Corn, Black Bean, and Cherry Tomato Salad with Southwest Chipotle Chile–Grilled Chicken

Because Southwest Chipotle Chile–Grilled Chicken is so flavorful and easy to make, I find myself wanting to cook extra and have it for another dinner. I've sliced it and put it in tacos, and I've cubed it and made a quasi–Southwest Cobb salad, changing the cheese from Roquefort to pepper Jack, and using the vinaigrette in this recipe. Here, I am taking advantage of two recipes in this book and combining them for a colorful, big-tasting salad. Plan ahead so you have leftovers of both the chicken and the bean salad for this quick weeknight meal.

	¼	CUP EXTRA-VIRGIN OLIVE OIL
	1	TABLESPOON CIDER VINEGAR
	1	TEASPOON WHOLE-GRAIN MUSTARD
VINAIGRETTE	½	TEASPOON MINCED CANNED CHIPOTLE CHILES IN ADOBO SAUCE
	½	TEASPOON KOSHER OR SEA SALT
	½	TEASPOON SUGAR
	¼	TEASPOON FRESHLY GROUND PEPPER
	2	HEARTS OF ROMAINE LETTUCE, TORN INTO BITE-SIZED PIECES
	¼	CUP LOOSELY PACKED FRESH CILANTRO LEAVES, PLUS 2 TABLESPOONS CHOPPED FOR GARNISH
[SERVES 4]	2	CUPS GRILLED SWEET CORN, BLACK BEAN, AND CHERRY TOMATO SALAD (PAGE 173)
	4	SOUTHWEST CHIPOTLE CHILE–GRILLED CHICKEN BREASTS (PAGE 111), CUT INTO ¼-INCH-THICK SLICES

To make the vinaigrette, in a small bowl, whisk together the olive oil, vinegar, mustard, chiles, salt, sugar, and pepper. Taste and adjust the seasoning.

To assemble the salad, place the romaine and ¼ cup cilantro in a large bowl. Give the vinaigrette a last-minute stir, then drizzle it over the greens and toss just until coated. Divide the greens among dinner plates. Spoon about ⅓ cup of the corn salad over each bed of greens. Arrange overlapping chicken slices over the top. Garnish with the chopped cilantro and serve immediately.

Grilled Salmon with Spinach, Orange, and Red Onion Salad

Spinach colorfully mixed with red bell pepper, thinly sliced red onion, and navel orange segments makes a satisfying salad on its own, but when freshly grilled salmon is placed on top, you have a main-course salad worth raving about. Save time and buy the packaged prewashed, trimmed baby spinach. The greens stay fresh for several days in the refrigerator. This salad does double duty, great for a weeknight meal or a Sunday brunch.

	4	PORTIONS ALDER-PLANKED SALMON WITH FRESH HERBS (PAGE 86)
	7	CUPS (ABOUT 6 OUNCES) LIGHTLY PACKED BABY SPINACH LEAVES
	1	CUP THINLY SLICED RED ONION
[SERVES 4]	1	RED BELL PEPPER, HALVED LENGTHWISE, SEEDED, DERIBBED, AND CUT INTO LONG, NARROW STRIPS
	2	NAVEL ORANGES, PEELED AND WHITE PITH REMOVED, SEPARATED INTO SEGMENTS
	¼	CUP EXTRA-VIRGIN OLIVE OIL
	1	TABLESPOON BALSAMIC VINEGAR
VINAIGRETTE	1	TEASPOON WHOLE-GRAIN MUSTARD
	½	TEASPOON SUGAR
	½	TEASPOON KOSHER OR SEA SALT
		FRESHLY GROUND PEPPER

Remove the salmon from the refrigerator 20 to 30 minutes before serving.

Place the spinach, onion, bell pepper, and orange segments in a large salad bowl.

To make the vinaigrette, in a small jar with a tight-fitting lid, combine the olive oil, vinegar, mustard, sugar, salt, and pepper to taste. Cover tightly and shake vigorously to blend. Taste and adjust the seasoning.

When ready to serve, give the vinaigrette a last-minute shake and pour over the salad. Toss gently to coat evenly. Divide the salad among dinner plates. Place a salmon fillet in the center of each plate, on top of the salad, and serve immediately.

Hearts of Romaine Caesar Salad with Lemon-Marinated Chicken and Chunky Parmesan Croutons

If you have four leftover Lemon-Marinated Chicken Breasts (page 116) in your refrigerator, this main-course salad is almost made. Unlike most Caesar salads that have predictable torn lettuce leaves, this one uses the tender inner greens and ultracrisp hearts of romaine piled high on the plate like canoes. Think of this salad as finger food—delightfully eaten one leaf at a time.

DRESSING

1 VERY FRESH LARGE EGG IN THE SHELL
1 TABLESPOON MINCED GARLIC
2 OIL-PACKED ANCHOVY FILLETS, PATTED DRY AND MINCED
¾ TEASPOON KOSHER OR SEA SALT
2 TABLESPOONS FRESH LEMON JUICE
½ CUP EXTRA-VIRGIN OLIVE OIL
¼ CUP FRESHLY GRATED PARMIGIANO-REGGIANO CHEESE

[SERVES 4]

1¼ CUPS HOMEMADE OR STORE-BOUGHT LARGE CROUTONS
5 HEARTS OF ROMAINE LETTUCE, LEAVES SEPARATED AND LEFT WHOLE
4 LEMON-MARINATED CHICKEN BREASTS (PAGE 116), THINLY SLICED
FRESHLY GRATED PARMIGIANO-REGGIANO CHEESE FOR GARNISH
FRESHLY GROUND PEPPER

To make the dressing, rinse the egg in warm water, and then set it in a mug. Add boiling water to cover and let stand for 1 minute. Immediately run cold water into the mug until the egg can be easily handled.

In a small bowl, whisk together the garlic, anchovies, salt, and lemon juice. Peel the egg, add it to the bowl, and whisk until thick, about 1 minute. Slowly drizzle in the oil, whisking vigorously to thicken. Whisk in the ¼ cup cheese. Taste and adjust the seasoning.

To assemble the salad, pour half of the dressing in the bottom of an oversized bowl. Add the croutons and toss until evenly coated. Add the lettuce and the remaining dressing and toss just until coated. Divide among dinner plates. Arrange the chicken slices over the top. Garnish with cheese and top with a few grinds of pepper. Serve immediately.

Grilled Lamb and Lemon Couscous Salad
with Apricots and Currants

Quick-cooking couscous is always on my pantry shelf, and this recipe illustrates why. In no more than ten minutes, I can have the dried, granular semolina rehydrated, fluffed, and ready to serve. I like to dress it with a citrus vinaigrette and add fresh and/or dried fruits, savory herbs, and sometimes nuts for a contrasting texture. Pair the salad with slices of grilled meat—especially tasty with lamb—and you have a speedy weeknight main course.

	1	CUP QUICK-COOKING COUSCOUS (SEE COOK'S NOTE, PAGE 170)
[SERVES 4]	½	CUP DRIED CURRANTS
	1¼	CUPS BOILING WATER
	6	TABLESPOONS EXTRA-VIRGIN OLIVE OIL
	2½	TABLESPOONS FRESH LEMON JUICE
VINAIGRETTE	2	CLOVES GARLIC, MINCED
	½	TEASPOON KOSHER OR SEA SALT
	½	TEASPOON FRESHLY GROUND PEPPER
	2	TABLESPOONS MINCED FRESH FLAT-LEAF PARSLEY
	6	RIPE APRICOTS, HALVED, PITTED, AND CUT INTO THIN WEDGES
	2	GREEN ONIONS, INCLUDING GREEN TOPS, THINLY SLICED
	2	LAMB STEAKS WITH *HERBES DE PROVENCE* SPICE RUB (PAGE 56), WARMED AND CUT ACROSS THE GRAIN INTO ¼-INCH-THICK SLICES

In a 3-quart heatproof bowl, stir together the couscous and currants, and pour the boiling water over the top. Cover with plastic wrap and let steep until the couscous is tender and the currants are plump, about 10 minutes.

Meanwhile, make the vinaigrette: In a small bowl, whisk together the olive oil, lemon juice, garlic, salt, and pepper. Taste and adjust the seasoning.

To assemble the salad, fluff the couscous with a fork, give the vinaigrette a last-minute stir, and gently blend it into the couscous. Stir in the parsley, apricots, and green onions. Divide the couscous among warmed dinner plates, and arrange the lamb slices over the top. Serve immediately.

Shrimp and Orzo Salad with Cherry Tomatoes, Green Onions, Feta, Kalamata Olives, and Lemon Vinaigrette

When I'm pressed for time, I love pasta recipes in which everything can be chopped and measured while the pasta cooks. If you have the leftover grilled shrimp on hand, this main-course salad requires only about ten minutes of preparation time and ten minutes of cooking time. I serve it with a loaf of crusty bread and open a bottle of crisp Italian white wine. Look for already-pitted Kalamata olives, which are sold in bulk or in jars and make a great pantry staple.

KOSHER OR SEA SALT

1¼ CUPS (ABOUT 8 OUNCES) ORZO (RICE-SHAPED PASTA)

3 TABLESPOONS EXTRA-VIRGIN OLIVE OIL

1 TABLESPOON FRESH LEMON JUICE

½ TEASPOON FRESHLY GROUND PEPPER

[SERVES 4] 12 CHERRY TOMATOES, QUARTERED

2 GREEN ONIONS, INCLUDING GREEN TOPS, THINLY SLICED

½ CUP PITTED AND HALVED KALAMATA OLIVES

4 OUNCES FETA CHEESE, CRUMBLED

12 OUNCES LARGE SHRIMP (26/30 COUNT) IN THE SHELL, PREPARED AS GARLIC AND SEA SALT PEEL 'N' EAT SHRIMP (PAGE 107), PEELED, TAILS REMOVED, AND HALVED LENGTHWISE

Fill a 3-quart saucepan two-thirds full of water and bring to a boil over high heat. Add 1 teaspoon salt to the boiling water, then add the orzo. Stir and cook the pasta until al dente (cooked through but still slightly chewy), 8 to 10 minutes. Drain the pasta, rinse with cold water, and drain thoroughly again.

Transfer the orzo to a large bowl and toss with the olive oil, lemon juice, and pepper. Add the tomatoes, green onions, olives, cheese, and shrimp and toss gently to combine. Taste and adjust the seasoning. Serve immediately.

Penne Pasta with Grilled Sweet Peppers, Grilled Onions, and Basil

When I see bushels of bright red, yellow, and orange peppers at the farmers' market, I can't resist. While one of each color looks good, two seem even better. I start thinking of a dinner menu that marries a mixed grill of olive oil–brushed vegetables with grilled chicken, chops, or steaks. But then I think about the possibilities for the extras. Grilling a couple of extra peppers and a sweet onion is the makings of an easy weeknight meal—this pasta dish!

KOSHER OR SEA SALT

1 POUND PENNE PASTA

⅓ CUP EXTRA-VIRGIN OLIVE OIL

1 RED BELL PEPPER, HALVED, SEEDED, DERIBBED, GRILLED, AND CHOPPED

1 YELLOW OR ORANGE BELL PEPPER, HALVED, SEEDED, DERIBBED, GRILLED, AND CHOPPED

[SERVES 4] 1 LARGE WALLA WALLA OR OTHER SWEET ONION, CUT CROSSWISE INTO ½-INCH-THICK SLICES, GRILLED, AND CHOPPED

½ PINT CHERRY TOMATOES, HALVED

¼ CUP COARSELY CHOPPED FRESH FLAT-LEAF PARSLEY

2 TABLESPOONS COARSELY CHOPPED FRESH BASIL

FRESHLY GROUND PEPPER

⅓ CUP FRESHLY GRATED PARMIGIANO-REGGIANO CHEESE

Fill an 8- to 10-quart stockpot two-thirds full of water and bring to a boil over high heat. Add 1 tablespoon salt to the boiling water, then add the pasta. Stir and cook the pasta until al dente (cooked through but still slightly chewy), about 10 minutes.

While the pasta is cooking, warm the olive oil in a large skillet over medium heat. Add the grilled peppers and onion and the cherry tomatoes. Stir gently until just heated through.

Drain the pasta and place it in a warmed serving bowl. Add the vegetables and all of the oil from the skillet and toss to combine. Sprinkle the parsley and basil over the top, season with salt and pepper, and again toss gently to combine. Garnish with the cheese and serve immediately.

Composed Greek Salad with Grilled Lamb, Heirloom Tomatoes, English Cucumbers, Olives, and Feta Chunks

This is the second main-course salad in this chapter that calls for grilled lamb. (Do you get the idea that I like lamb?) For this recipe, I have gone Greek and put together a lovely composed salad that is elegant on the platter but simple to make. Whisk together a lemon vinaigrette, slice tomatoes, cucumbers, and lamb, and dinner is made in no time. For an easy accompaniment, set out a warm, crusty artisanal bread or serve warm pita bread with store-bought hummus.

	½	CUP EXTRA-VIRGIN OLIVE OIL
	3½	TABLESPOONS FRESH LEMON JUICE
	2	LARGE CLOVES GARLIC, MINCED
VINAIGRETTE	¼	CUP MINCED FRESH FLAT-LEAF PARSLEY OR MINT
	¾	TEASPOON KOSHER OR SEA SALT
	½	TEASPOON SUGAR
	1	TEASPOON FRESHLY GROUND PEPPER
	8	WHOLE ROMAINE LEAVES, ENDS TRIMMED
	2	LARGE, RIPE TOMATOES, CORED AND THINLY SLICED
	1	SMALL ENGLISH CUCUMBER, THINLY SLICED
[SERVES 4]	2	MUSTARD-AND-ROSEMARY-CRUSTED LAMB STEAKS (PAGE 57), WARMED AND CUT ACROSS THE GRAIN INTO ¼-INCH-THICK SLICES
	½	CUP PITTED AND HALVED KALAMATA OLIVES
	6	OUNCES FRESH GOAT CHEESE, CRUMBLED

To make the vinaigrette, in a small jar with a tight-fitting lid, combine the olive oil, lemon juice, garlic, parsley, salt, sugar, and pepper. Cover tightly and shake vigorously to blend. Taste and adjust the seasoning.

To assemble the salad, arrange the romaine leaves, slightly overlapping them, on a large round or rectangular platter. Just below the top of the leaves, arrange the tomato slices, slightly overlapping them, in a row. Arrange the cucumbers in a similar way just below the tomatoes. Fan the lamb slices over the lettuce and below the cucumbers. Scatter the olives and goat cheese over the top. Give the vinaigrette a last-minute shake and drizzle over the salad. Serve immediately.

Grilled Lamb Burger and Pita Sandwich with Garlic-and-Mint Yogurt Sauce

Here is a casual sandwich supper that calls for extra lamb burgers you've grilled ahead. Use leftover yogurt sauce or make a half batch of the Garlic-and-Mint Yogurt Sauce (page 54). Romaine lettuce and roasted red peppers are just one way to stuff the pita sandwiches. You can use whatever vegetables you like, such as sliced cucumbers, sweet onions, or tomatoes; a mixture of romaine lettuce and fresh mint leaves; or grilled zucchini slices. Put out plenty of napkins. Buy some hummus and cut some crudités to serve along with the sandwiches.

[SERVES 4]

4   PITA BREADS, HALVED CROSSWISE
4   CHAR-GRILLED LAMB BURGERS (PAGE 54)
4   ROMAINE LEAVES, ENDS TRIMMED,
    CUT CROSSWISE INTO THIN RIBBONS
4   JARRED ROASTED RED PEPPERS, DRAINED AND BLOTTED DRY,
    CUT INTO LONG, NARROW STRIPS
¾   CUP GARLIC-AND-MINT YOGURT SAUCE (PAGE 54)

Preheat the oven to 250°F. Wrap the pita breads in aluminum foil. Cut the burgers in half horizontally, so you have 2 thin patties from each burger. Reform them as if they were uncut burgers, place them in a baking dish, and cover the dish with foil. Place the pitas and burgers in the oven until warmed, about 20 minutes.

To assemble the sandwiches, slip a thin burger into each pita half. Stuff some lettuce and red pepper strips inside each pita half and add a dollop of the yogurt sauce. Serve immediately.

Grilled Flank Steak Salad with Grilled New Potatoes and *Chimichurri*

This main-course salad brings together the big flavors of *Chimichurri* with warmed flank steak, slivers of sweet onion, and new potatoes to create a hearty meal. The sauce can be made while the potatoes are cooking, which makes the prep time less than a half hour. Although I have boiled new potatoes for this salad, you could cook an extra batch of New Potatoes Tossed with Extra-Virgin Olive Oil and *Fleur de Sel* (page 154) and use them instead.

[SERVES 4]

12 OUNCES NEW RED POTATOES

1 TEASPOON KOSHER OR SEA SALT

1 CUP *CHIMICHURRI* (PAGE 48)

1 GRILLED FLANK STEAK (PAGE 41),
WARMED AND CUT ACROSS THE GRAIN
INTO ¼-INCH-THICK SLICES

1 SMALL WALLA WALLA OR OTHER SWEET ONION,
CUT INTO PAPER-THIN WEDGES

Scrub the potatoes but leave the skins on. In a saucepan, combine the potatoes with water to cover by 1 inch. Add the salt and bring to a boil. Adjust the heat so the water just simmers, cover partially, and cook until tender when pierced with a fork, about 20 minutes. Drain, let cool slightly, and halve the potatoes.

While the potatoes are cooking, make the *Chimichurri*, and warm and slice the flank steak.

To assemble the salad, arrange the steak slices, slightly overlapping them, on 4 dinner plates, or arrange all of the steak on 1 large round or rectangular platter. Scatter the potatoes and onion over the steak. Drizzle the sauce over the salad and serve immediately.

Shrimp, Pineapple, and Anaheim Chile Salad with Avocado

Sometimes after work, neither wanting to fuss in the kitchen nor turn on the oven, I think about making a main-course salad or one-plate meal. With leftover spicy shrimp in the refrigerator, tasty and cold, I can "stretch" a small quantity of seafood into a dinner for four by adding a refreshing blend of citrus fruit, sweet red pepper, mild chiles, and avocado. This is a satisfying light summertime meal. Warm some tortillas to serve alongside.

	6	TABLESPOONS EXTRA-VIRGIN OLIVE OIL
	1½	TABLESPOONS FRESH LIME JUICE
	2	CLOVES GARLIC, MINCED
VINAIGRETTE	1½	TABLESPOONS MINCED FRESH CILANTRO
	½	TEASPOON KOSHER OR SEA SALT
	½	TEASPOON SUGAR
	½	TEASPOON FRESHLY GROUND PEPPER
	12	OUNCES CHILI-RUBBED SHRIMP (PAGE 101), HALVED CROSSWISE
	½	PINEAPPLE, PEELED, HALVED LENGTHWISE, CORED, AND CUT INTO ¾-INCH CUBES
[SERVES 4]	2	ANAHEIM CHILES, SEEDED, DERIBBED, AND CUT INTO ½-INCH DICE
	1	RED BELL PEPPER, SEEDED, DERIBBED, AND CUT INTO ½-INCH DICE
	8	OUTER LEAVES FROM 1 HEAD BUTTER LETTUCE
	2	LARGE HASS AVOCADOS, HALVED, PITTED, PEELED, AND CUT INTO ½-INCH CUBES

To make the vinaigrette, in a small jar with a tight-fitting lid, combine the olive oil, lime juice, garlic, cilantro, salt, sugar, and pepper. Cover tightly and shake vigorously to blend. Taste and adjust the seasoning.

Place the shrimp, pineapple, chiles, and bell pepper in a large bowl. Give the vinaigrette a last-minute shake, add to the bowl, and toss gently until evenly coated.

To assemble the salad, arrange the lettuce leaves, slightly overlapping them, on a large round or rectangular platter. Mound the shrimp mixture over the lettuce, and scatter the avocado over the top. Serve immediately.

FIRE-ROASTED FRUITS + OTHER SWEET TREATS

SEASONAL FRUITS GRILLED TO WARM, JUICY PERFECTION MAKE A DRAMATIC FINISH TO ANY MEAL—GRILLED OR NOT. I still remember the first time I grilled peaches that I bought at the farmers' market. They were firm but ripe and at the peak of the season, which in Oregon is mid-August to mid-September. They were as sweet as could be, freestone, and the size of a baseball. I halved them and let them macerate in a tropical syrup of rum, melted butter, and dark brown sugar. The sugar caramelized over the fire, incising beautiful grill marks across the golden fruits. Dessert became a lusty treat of two warm grilled peach halves nestled in a bowl with a big scoop of *dulce de leche* ice cream and some extra rum syrup drizzled over the top. It was an ooh-and-aah moment for everyone at the table, and it launched my quest to try to grill just about every fruit in the market.

I've filled this chapter with my favorite fruits to grill, and added in some other quick sweet treats. I'm in love with grilled pound cake, either plain or poppy seed. Brushed with melted butter and grilled just long enough to toast and warm the slices, pound cake turns into a delectable treat when topped with fresh fruit and a mountain of whipped cream or crème fraîche. Now, that's an easy dessert to make—especially when a good bakery does the baking! Here are a few tips and guidelines for grilling fruit successfully.

FIRST, start with a clean, medium or medium-hot, well-oiled grill surface. Even small bits of charred food left on the grill grate will stick to the cut side of fruits and tear the flesh when you try to move them, especially bananas. Preheat the grill; brush the grill grate so it's clean, clean, clean; and oil the grate thoroughly so it is well coated and slick.

SECOND, have the fruit at room temperature. If it has been refrigerated, remove it an hour or so prior to grilling. After washing the fruit, blot it dry with paper towels so there is no residual moisture. This way, for the recipes in which the fruit is macerated, the flavored liquids won't be diluted by excess moisture on the fruit, and for those recipes where butter is brushed on the fruit, the melted butter won't congeal due to the fruit being cold.

THIRD, with the exception of the apples, pineapple, and nectarines for the crisp, all the fruits in this chapter are grilled over direct heat with the grill uncovered. Because fruits are rich in natural sugars, they caramelize quickly. You must pay careful attention to achieve beautiful grill marks and bronzing without the sugars burning. It is sometimes a good idea to create a cool zone (see page 21) before the fruit goes on the grill, so you have the option of moving the fruit to a cool area to finish cooking. This is especially true for large peaches and nectarines. Searing caramelizes the fruit, but sometimes it still needs extra time to soften. Moving the fruit away from the direct flame and covering the grill gives it that extra time.

FOURTH, even if the fruit has been macerated in a butter-based sauce, be sure it is well buttered before it goes on the grill. Bananas are prone to sticking and need a good slathering with butter before the cut sides are grilled. The same is true for slices of pound cake.

FINALLY, use the right tools for turning fruits and for ensuring you get them off the grill in time. Always use tongs, never a two-pronged fork, to move or turn the fruit, because a fork can tear the flesh. For slices of pineapple or pound cake, use a wide spatula in tandem with tongs for ease. A grill basket or grill grid (see page 26) is the perfect tool for cooking small fruits, such as figs and plums. I arrange all the fruit, cut side down, on the basket or grid before I set it on the grill grate. It makes it easier to control the grilling time, because you can lift the grid or basket off the grill as soon as the fruit is caramelized, rather than remove the fruit piece by piece.

Plums with Grand Marnier and Mango Sorbet

As with the other grilled fruit in this chapter, grilled plums are divine whether served for dessert, as this recipe shows, or served as a sweet side to grilled meats, especially pork, chicken, and salmon. Plan to grill extra and serve them with Salmon Grilled on a Bed of Herbs (page 89), or combine them in a salad with mesclun, crumbled goat cheese, and toasted nuts and toss with Walnut Vinaigrette (page 176).

[SERVES 4]

2 TABLESPOONS UNSALTED BUTTER, MELTED
2 TABLESPOONS SUGAR
4 FIRM BUT RIPE PLUMS, HALVED AND PITTED
1 PINT MANGO SORBET
GRAND MARNIER FOR DRIZZLING

Prepare a medium fire in a charcoal grill or preheat a gas grill on medium.

In a small bowl, combine the butter and sugar and stir until the sugar is dissolved. Place the plums in a large bowl. Using a rubber spatula, gently stir in the butter mixture until the fruit is well coated.

Oil the grill grate, or arrange the plums, cut side down, on an oiled grill grid or basket. Grill the plums directly over the medium fire just until grill marks are etched across the fruit, about 2 minutes. Turn and grill, skin side down, just until tender, about 3 minutes longer. Brush with the butter mixture remaining in the bowl while the fruit is cooking.

To serve, cut each plum half into 3 wedges. Place 2 scoops of mango sorbet in each dessert bowl, and arrange the plum wedges on top. Drizzle with Grand Marnier. Serve immediately.

Pears with Cognac-Soaked Currants

Grilled pears make a splendid dessert, of course, but you should also think about grilled pears as a substitute for potatoes the next time you are grilling chicken or pork. These pears would be fabulous with Chicken Thighs with Espresso-Cardamom Rub (page 121) or Pork Tenderloin with Apricot-Mustard Glaze (page 70). Anjou pears are the best choice for grilling, as they hold their good texture. Comice and Bartlett pears turn mealy on the grill, while Bosc pears are better saved for poaching.

[SERVES 4]

⅓   CUP DRIED CURRANTS

¼   CUP COGNAC OR ANOTHER BRANDY

PINCH OF FRESHLY GROUND PEPPER

4   FIRM BUT RIPE ANJOU PEARS

4   TABLESPOONS (½ STICK) UNSALTED BUTTER, MELTED

Prepare a medium-hot fire in a charcoal grill or preheat a gas grill on medium-high.

In a small bowl, combine the currants, Cognac, and pepper and let macerate until ready to serve.

Peel the pears and cut in half lengthwise. Using a melon baller or paring knife, remove the core, leaving a gumball-sized hole. Place on a rimmed baking sheet and brush all over with the butter.

Oil the grill grate. Arrange the pears, cut side down, directly over the medium-hot fire and grill until they begin to turn golden brown and grill marks are etched across the fruit, about 3 minutes. Turn and grill, skin side down, just until tender, about 3 minutes longer.

To serve, arrange 2 pear halves, cut side up, on each dessert plate or bowl. Spoon the Cognac-soaked currants over the top. Serve immediately.

Rum-Glazed Grilled Pineapple
with *Dulce de Leche* Ice Cream

I used grilled pineapple as a sweet accompaniment to savory grilled meat in Jerk Pork Tenderloin with Grilled Pineapple (page 67), but the fruit develops such a terrific caramelized flavor that I wanted to turn it into a dessert, too. Although the flavor combinations are endless, I happen to be a big fan of grilled pineapple with dark rum and caramel ice cream. But don't stop there. Consider grilled pineapple with rum-raisin ice cream, go tropical and serve it topped with shredded coconut and with coconut ice cream on the side, or go simple and serve it with a scoop of vanilla ice cream.

[SERVES 4]

3	TABLESPOONS UNSALTED BUTTER, MELTED
1	TABLESPOON PACKED DARK BROWN SUGAR
¼	CUP DARK RUM, PLUS MORE FOR DRIZZLING (OPTIONAL)
¼	TEASPOON FRESHLY GROUND PEPPER
1	RIPE PINEAPPLE, PEELED, HALVED LENGTHWISE, AND CUT CROSSWISE INTO ½-INCH-THICK SLICES (DO NOT CORE)
1	PINT *DULCE DE LECHE* ICE CREAM

Prepare a medium-hot fire in a charcoal grill or preheat a gas grill on medium-high.

In a small bowl, combine the butter, sugar, rum, and pepper. Stir to dissolve the sugar. Arrange the pineapple slices in a single layer on a large, rimmed baking sheet and brush the slices on both sides with the butter mixture. Set aside.

Oil the grill grate. Place the pineapple directly over the medium-hot fire. Cover the grill and grill the pineapple, turning once, until grill marks appear on both sides and the pineapple is golden and tender when pierced with a knife, about 3 minutes per side.

To serve, divide the pineapple slices among dessert plates or bowls. Place a scoop or two of ice cream on top of each serving. Drizzle with additional rum, if desired. Serve immediately.

Grill-Roasted Apples with Maple Syrup, Cinnamon Sticks, and Golden Raisins

In the late summer and early fall, when apples are at their best, I love to grill-roast them. This dessert takes little preparation, and the apples can bake while the embers are low and you are eating dinner. For me, grill-roasted apples are homey and satisfying, and signal the beginning of fall and the glories of the harvest. Use any good baking apple, especially local varieties; just make sure the apples are firm. After trying lots of apple varieties while testing this recipe, I consistently preferred Golden Delicious for its texture and flavor. Gala, Pippin, Winesap, and Cortland apples work well, too. Avoid Red Delicious for baking, as the texture is too dry. Although I recommend serving the apples with a spoonful of cream, vanilla ice cream is always good, too.

[SERVES 4]

4	BAKING APPLES
¼	CUP GOLDEN RAISINS
4	CINNAMON STICKS, EACH 3 TO 4 INCHES LONG
4	TABLESPOONS (½ STICK) UNSALTED BUTTER, MELTED AND KEPT WARM
¼	CUP PURE MAPLE SYRUP
½	TEASPOON GROUND CINNAMON
¼	TEASPOON FRESHLY GRATED NUTMEG
⅓	CUP HEAVY (WHIPPING) CREAM (OPTIONAL)

Prepare a medium-hot fire in a charcoal grill or preheat a gas grill on medium-high.

Place 4 sheets of heavy-duty aluminum foil, each about 12 inches long, on a work surface. Core the apples with an apple corer or a vegetable peeler to make a straight, neatly cored-out section from the stem end to within about ¹/₄ inch of the blossom end. (Be careful not to cut through the blossom end, or the butter will leak out.) With the tip of a paring knife, and starting about one-third of the way down from the stem end, make a shallow incision in the skin of the apple, cutting completely around the diameter. (This technique allows the apples to expand, but not burst, while grill-roasting or baking.)

Drop the raisins into the hollowed cores. Lightly push a cinnamon stick into each hollowed core, just enough to secure it. In a small bowl, stir together the butter, maple syrup, cinnamon, and nutmeg.

Fold up the sheet of foil around each apple, leaving the top open. Pour the butter mixture down the hollowed cores and over the apples, dividing it evenly and using all of it. Press the foil around the top of each apple to seal it, leaving the top of the cinnamon stick exposed.

To create a cool zone, bank the coals to one side of the grill or turn off one of the burners.

Place the apple packages directly on the grill grate on the cool side of the grill, so the apples grill-roast over indirect heat. Cover and grill until the apples are tender when pierced with a knife, 20 to 30 minutes. (Timing will vary depending on the size and ripeness of the apples.)

Use a large spoon to transfer the apples from their foil packages to individual bowls, spooning any juices over the top. Spoon a generous tablespoon of cream over the top of each apple, if desired. Serve immediately.

Bananas Slicked with Rum and Molasses

Use this recipe as the basis for a sensational dessert, such as Grilled Banana Split Sundaes (page 210), or serve grilled bananas as an accompaniment to grilled meat or poultry. For example, consider accompanying the Jerk Pork Tenderloin (page 67) with grilled bananas instead of grilled pineapple, or serve them alongside Orange-and-Chipotle-Rubbed Chicken Breasts (page 117).

[SERVES 4]

3	TABLESPOONS UNSALTED BUTTER, MELTED AND KEPT WARM
2	TABLESPOONS UNSULFURED MOLASSES
1	TABLESPOON DARK RUM
4	FIRM BUT RIPE BANANAS, UNPEELED, HALVED LENGTHWISE

Prepare a medium-hot fire in a charcoal grill or preheat a gas grill on medium-high.

In a small bowl, stir together 1 tablespoon of the butter with the molasses and rum. Set aside. Arrange the bananas on a rimmed baking sheet, and brush their cut side with the remaining 2 tablespoons butter.

Oil the grill grate. Arrange the bananas, cut side down, directly over the medium-hot fire. Grill the bananas until they begin to turn golden brown and grill marks are etched across the fruit, about 2 minutes. Turn skin side down and grill just until tender when pierced with a knife, about 2 minutes longer.

Transfer the bananas to the rimmed baking sheet. The bananas can either be served in their skins or carefully scooped out with a spatula. Brush the fruit with the molasses mixture. Arrange on dessert plates and serve immediately.

Grilled Banana Split Sundaes

This recipe is really a make-your-own creation. I'm giving you directions on the crucial step of grilling the bananas, but everything else about these sundaes is personal preference. Select your favorite ice creams (mine would be chocolate, chocolate, and more chocolate), and pick your favorite sauces and toppings. The size and style of the sundaes are up to you. This is a great dessert for a party, especially if children are part of the group, but it is also quick fun for a special weeknight dessert.

[SERVES 4]

4	FIRM BUT RIPE BANANAS, UNPEELED, HALVED LENGTHWISE
4	TABLESPOONS (½ STICK) UNSALTED BUTTER, MELTED
3	PINTS OF YOUR FAVORITE ICE CREAMS
¾	CUP DARK CHOCOLATE SAUCE, WARMED
½	CUP CARAMEL SAUCE, WARMED
½	CUP TOASTED PECANS
½	CUP CHOPPED CANDY BAR SUCH AS HEATH BAR OR NESTLÉ CRUNCH (OPTIONAL)
	WHIPPED CREAM FOR SERVING

Prepare a medium-hot fire in a charcoal grill or preheat a gas grill on medium-high.

Arrange the bananas on a rimmed baking sheet and brush the cut side with the butter.

Oil the grill grate. Arrange the bananas, cut side down, directly over the medium-hot fire. Grill until they begin to turn golden brown and grill marks are etched across the fruit, about 2 minutes. Turn skin side down and grill just until tender when pierced with a knife, about 2 minutes longer.

To assemble the sundaes, place 2 or 3 scoops of ice cream in each dessert bowl. Slip the bananas out of their skins and arrange 2 halves in each bowl, placing them along either side of the ice cream. Drizzle the chocolate and caramel sauces over the ice creams. Sprinkle the nuts and candy, if desired, over the top, and add a dollop of whipped cream. Serve immediately.

Peaches or Nectarines with a Brown Sugar–Brandy Glaze

As with many other fruits, including figs and plums, grilled peaches and nectarines can be used as either a sweet accompaniment to savory foods, such as Latin-Rubbed Pork Tenderloin (page 66), or as the basis for a splendid dessert, such as Peaches with Raspberries and Raspberry Swirl Ice Cream (page 214). Grill extra and use them sliced in a salad with spinach or arugula or served alongside a bowl of granola and yogurt for breakfast.

[SERVES 4]

2   TABLESPOONS UNSALTED BUTTER, MELTED
2   TABLESPOONS PACKED DARK BROWN SUGAR
¼   CUP BRANDY
4   FIRM BUT RIPE FREESTONE PEACHES OR NECTARINES,
     HALVED AND PITTED

Prepare a medium fire in a charcoal grill or preheat a gas grill on medium.

In a small bowl, combine the butter, sugar, and brandy. Stir to dissolve the sugar. Place the fruit in a large bowl. Using a rubber spatula, gently stir in the brandy mixture until the fruit is well coated.

Oil the grill grate. Arrange the fruit, cut side down, directly over the medium fire and grill until it begins to turn golden brown and grill marks appear, about 3 minutes. Turn skin side down and grill just until tender when pierced with a knife, about 3 minutes longer. As the fruit cooks, brush it with the brandy mixture remaining in the bowl.

To serve, arrange 2 halves, cut side up, on each dessert plate or bowl, and drizzle any of the remaining brandy mixture over the top. Serve immediately.

Dark Chocolate S'Mores Sundaes

In 2002, Karen Brooks and I wrote *Dressed to Grill,* a sassy girl's grill book. We knew we had to bring back our Girl Scout days and make a fabulous dessert with s'mores. We wanted to go beyond the two graham crackers, split Hershey's bar, and toasted marshmallows, to give our readers an updated, urban girl's idea of this treasured campfire dessert. The recipe is so good I am including it in this book. It's a s'mores sundae with first-rate ice cream or sorbet, a good-quality chocolate sauce, toasted marshmallows, and chocolate graham crackers.

	1	PINT COCONUT ICE CREAM OR SORBET
	⅓	CUP COARSELY CHOPPED BITTERSWEET CHOCOLATE
[SERVES 4]	12	MARSHMALLOWS
	4	METAL SKEWERS
	1	CUP GOOD-QUALITY CHOCOLATE SAUCE, WARMED
	4	CHOCOLATE GRAHAM CRACKERS

Remove the ice cream or sorbet from the freezer and let stand at room temperature until soft enough to run a spoon through it, 10 to 20 minutes. Transfer to a medium bowl. Stir in the chopped chocolate. Repack the ice cream or sorbet into the carton. Freeze for several hours or up to overnight.

Prepare a hot fire in a charcoal grill or preheat a gas grill on high.

Thread 3 marshmallows onto each skewer. Arrange the skewers directly over the hot fire and toast the marshmallows, turning as needed, until puffed and toasty brown, 2 to 3 minutes.

To assemble the sundaes, place 1 big scoop of ice cream or sorbet in each dessert bowl. Drizzle 2 tablespoons of the chocolate sauce over each scoop. Top each serving with 3 toasted marshmallows and place a graham cracker on the side. Serve immediately.

Peaches with Raspberries and Raspberry Swirl Ice Cream

Here I have taken the classic peach Melba dessert and kicked it up a notch by topping warm grilled peaches with scoops of rich raspberry swirl ice cream and a scattering of summer's best raspberries. To give this dish an elegant touch, drizzle it with framboise. Oregon's award-winning Clear Creek Distillery makes an especially fine version of the eau de vie, using some eighty pounds of the state's excellent raspberries to make a single small bottle of framboise!

[SERVES 4]

3   TABLESPOONS UNSALTED BUTTER, MELTED
2   TABLESPOONS SUGAR
4   FIRM BUT RIPE FREESTONE PEACHES, HALVED AND PITTED
1   PINT RASPBERRY SWIRL ICE CREAM
1   PINT RASPBERRIES
FRAMBOISE FOR DRIZZLING (OPTIONAL)

Prepare a medium fire in a charcoal grill or preheat a gas grill on medium.

In a small bowl, combine the butter and sugar and stir until the sugar is dissolved. Place the peaches in a large bowl. Using a rubber spatula, gently stir in the butter mixture until the fruit is well coated.

Oil the grill grate. Arrange the peaches, cut side down, directly over the medium fire and grill until they begin to turn golden brown and grill marks are etched across the fruit, about 3 minutes. Turn and grill, skin side down, just until tender when pierced with a knife, about 3 minutes longer. As the peaches cook, brush them with the butter mixture remaining in the bowl.

To serve, arrange 2 peach halves, cut side up, in each dessert bowl. Place a scoop or two of ice cream on the peaches, and scatter the raspberries over the top. Drizzle with framboise, if desired. Serve immediately.

Grilled Pound Cake Slices
with Strawberries and Crème Chantilly

What could be simpler and yummier than buying an all-butter pound cake from the bakery, cutting it into thick slices, grilling them, and serving the cake with fresh-from-the-farmers'-market strawberries and whipped cream? I've made this dessert with homemade pound cake, bakery-shop cake, and even frozen Sara Lee pound cake. Grilling makes the pound cake warm, crisp, and toasted. Grill extra slices for breakfast!

[SERVES 4]

4	THICK SLICES STORE-BOUGHT POUND CAKE
4	TABLESPOONS (½ STICK) UNSALTED BUTTER, MELTED
1	PINT STRAWBERRIES, HULLED AND SLICED
2	TEASPOONS GRANULATED SUGAR
¾	CUP HEAVY (WHIPPING) CREAM
½	TEASPOON PURE VANILLA EXTRACT
1	TABLESPOON POWDERED SUGAR

Prepare a medium fire in a charcoal grill or preheat a gas grill on medium.

Arrange the pound cake in a single layer on a large, rimmed baking sheet and brush the slices on both sides with the butter.

While the grill is heating, in a bowl, toss the strawberries with the granulated sugar. Set aside. In another bowl, combine the cream, vanilla, and powdered sugar. Use a whisk or electric mixer to whip the cream until soft peaks form. Cover and refrigerate until ready to serve.

Oil the grill grate. Arrange the cake slices directly over the medium fire and grill, turning once, until grill marks appear on both sides and the slices are warmed through and toasted, 1 to 2 minutes per side.

To serve, place a slice of grilled cake on each dessert plate. Spoon the strawberries over the top, and add a dollop of whipped cream. Serve immediately.

Grilled Lemon–Poppy Seed Pound Cake with Summer Berries and Crème Fraîche

Give me chocolate or give me blueberries—wasn't that a famous quote? Perhaps not, but blueberries are among my favorite ingredients when it comes to creating desserts. I eat blueberries every day when they are in season, and I'm always thinking up ways to pair them with other ingredients. This recipe with grilled lemon–poppy seed pound cake is a winner. Make this dessert for a family dinner, make it for a big party, or make it for brunch—everyone loves it. In fact, grill extra slices and keep extra berries on hand, because there will be requests for seconds.

[SERVES 4]

4   THICK SLICES STORE-BOUGHT LEMON–POPPY SEED POUND CAKE
4   TABLESPOONS (½ STICK) UNSALTED BUTTER, MELTED
½   PINT BLUEBERRIES
½   PINT RASPBERRIES
¾   CUP CRÈME FRAÎCHE

Prepare a medium fire in a charcoal grill or preheat a gas grill on medium.

Arrange the pound cake in a single layer on a rimmed baking sheet and brush the slices on both sides with the butter.

Oil the grill grate. Arrange the cake slices directly over the medium fire and grill, turning once, until grill marks appear on both sides and the slices are warmed through and toasted, 1 to 2 minutes per side.

To serve, place a slice of grilled cake on each dessert plate. Spoon the berries over the top, and add a dollop of crème fraîche. Serve immediately.

Grilled Nectarine and Blueberry Crisp

I love to make fruit crisps in the summer and fall. I pair whatever fruits inspire me at the farmers' market—peaches and raspberries, nectarines and blueberries, cherries and apricots, pears and currants—grilled or not, so I have a total of 6 cups filling. Then, I make a triple or quadruple batch of the topping. I measure out about 2½ cups of topping per crisp, set aside one batch for the crisp at hand, and then put the other portions in separate freezer bags (labeled, of course), so they are ready to use for future crisps.

[SERVES 4]

4	TABLESPOONS (½ STICK) UNSALTED BUTTER, MELTED
2	TABLESPOONS PACKED LIGHT BROWN SUGAR
6	FIRM BUT RIPE NECTARINES, HALVED AND PITTED
1½	CUPS BLUEBERRIES
2	TABLESPOONS GRANULATED SUGAR
1	TABLESPOON QUICK-COOKING TAPIOCA, UNCOOKED

TOPPING

¾	CUP OLD-FASHIONED ROLLED OATS
⅔	CUP PACKED LIGHT BROWN SUGAR
½	CUP ALL-PURPOSE FLOUR
¾	TEASPOON GROUND CINNAMON
¼	TEASPOON KOSHER OR SEA SALT
½	CUP (1 STICK) ICE-COLD UNSALTED BUTTER, CUT INTO SMALL PIECES
½	CUP SLICED, UNBLANCHED ALMONDS

1	PINT VANILLA ICE CREAM

Prepare a medium fire in a charcoal grill or preheat a gas grill on medium.

In a large bowl, combine 3 tablespoons of the butter with the 2 tablespoons brown sugar and stir until the sugar is dissolved. Place the nectarines in the bowl. Using a rubber spatula, gently stir until the fruit is well coated with the butter mixture.

Oil the grill grate. Arrange the nectarines, cut side down, directly over the medium fire. Grill until they begin to turn golden brown and light grill marks are etched across the fruit, about 2 minutes. Turn skin side down and grill until barely tender, about 2 minutes longer. As the nectarines cook, brush them with the butter mixture remaining in the bowl. Transfer the fruit to a cutting board and reserve the bowl used for making the filling.

Preheat the oven to 400°F. Butter a shallow 2-quart baking dish with the remaining 1 tablespoon butter.

Cut the nectarines into wedges and place in the reserved bowl along with the blueberries, granulated sugar, and tapioca. Using a rubber spatula, stir gently to combine. Transfer to the prepared baking dish.

To make the topping, in a bowl, stir together the oats, $^2/_3$ cup brown sugar, the flour, cinnamon, and salt. Scatter the butter over the flour mixture. Using a pastry cutter or your fingertips, blend the butter into the oats mixture until the mixture is crumbly and the size of coarse crumbs. Mix in the almonds.

Sprinkle the topping evenly over the fruit filling. Bake the crisp until the top is nicely browned and the fruit is tender when pierced with a fork, about 30 minutes. Serve warm with a scoop of vanilla ice cream.

Figs with *Fromage Blanc* and Honey

When I see figs at the farmers' market, my mind starts buzzing with possibilities. Do I grill the fruit and turn it into a luscious dessert, or should I serve the grilled figs as part of a salad, such as Grilled Fig and Green Bean Salad with Walnut Vinaigrette (page 176)? I like to eat figs fresh, but when they pick up a caramelized flavor from being seared on the grill, they become irresistible. This recipe uses *fromage blanc*, a soft, fresh cream cheese, available at cheese shops or gourmet grocery stores. A firm sheep's milk cheese, such as Spanish Manchego, is also delicious paired with grilled figs for dessert.

[SERVES 4]

8 RIPE BLACK MISSION FIGS, HALVED LENGTHWISE
2 TABLESPOONS UNSALTED BUTTER, MELTED
1 CUP *FROMAGE BLANC*, AT ROOM TEMPERATURE
¼ CUP HONEY

Prepare a medium fire in a charcoal grill or preheat a gas grill on medium.

Brush the figs on all sides with the butter.

Oil the grill grate, or arrange the figs, cut side down, on an oiled grill grid or basket. Grill the figs directly over the medium fire just until grill marks appear, about 1 minute. Turn and grill until tender but still firm when pierced with a knife, about 1 minute longer.

To serve, arrange 4 fig halves, cut side up, on each dessert plate or bowl. Spoon a large dollop of *fromage blanc* alongside, and drizzle the honey over the top. Serve immediately.

SOURCES

GRILLS AND ACCESSORIES

There are many manufacturers of outdoor grills. I've listed a few here, but it is best to look at Web sites online to get a sense of price, features, and quality, and then visit your local dealers.

Char-Broil/W.C. Bradley
P.O. Box 1240
Columbus, Georgia 31902-1240
800-352-4111
www.charbroil.com

DCS (Dynamic Cooking Systems)
5800 Skylab Road
Huntington Beach, California 92647
800-433-8466
www.dcsappliances.com

Grill Lover's Catalogue
P.O. Box 1300
Columbus, Georgia 31902-1300
800-241-8981
www.grilllovers.com

KitchenAid
P.O. Box 218
St. Joseph, Michigan 49084
800-422-1230
www.kitchenaid.com

Weber-Stephen Products Company
200 East Daniels Road
Palatine, Illinois 60067-6266
800-446-1071
800-GRILLOUT
(open 364 days a year, 24/7)
www.weber.com

CHARCOAL AND WOOD

American Wood Products
9540 Riggs Street
Overland Park, Kansas 66212
800-223-9046

The Kingsford Products Company
www.kingsford.com

People's Woods/Nature's Own
51 Graystone Street
Warwick, Rhode Island 02887
800-443-6450
www.peopleswoods.com

GRILLING PLANKS, CEDAR SHEETS, GRILL TOOLS, ETC.

Barbecuewood.com
800-DRYWOOD (379-9663)
www.barbecuewood.com

BBQ Pro Shop
(Small quantities of cedar sheets plus grills, accessories, etc.)
935 Northwoods Road
Deerfield, Illinois 60015
866-201-0696 (U.S. only)
www.bbqproshop.com

Grate Chef Grill Wipes
(Disposable grill wipes for oiling the grill)
P.O. Box 1504
Dacula, Georgia 30019
www.gratechef.com

Korin Japanese Trading Company
(Large quantities of cedar sheets)
57 Warren Street
New York, New York 10007
800-626-2172
www.korin.com

OUTDOOR COOKING

Turkey Cannon
(Replaces the beer can for beer can chicken)
P.O. Box 4028
Logan, Utah 84323
866-674-0538
www.outdoorcooking.com

Wild River Grilling
(Quality grilling planks as well as wild salmon)
602 Langdale Drive
Fort Collins, Colorado 80526
866-894-WILD (9453)
www.wildrivergrilling.com

MEATS

Five Herds Trading Co.
(Good source for bison)
P.O. Box 16490
Golden, Colorado 80402
888-543-7371
www.fiveherds.com

McGonigle's Market
(Great source for dry-aged beef)
1307 W. 79th Street
Kansas City, Missouri 64114
888-783-2540
www.mcgonigles.com

Montana-Wyoming Buffalo Company
422 N. Excelsior Avenue
Butte, Montana 59701
406-723-4564
www.westernbuffalo.com

FISH

Legal Sea Foods
One Seafood Way
Boston, Massachusetts 02210
800-343-5804
http://shop.legalseafoods.com

Troller Point Fisheries
(Alaskan wild salmon)
907-344-1866
www.trollerpoint.com

Vital Choice Seafood
(Wild salmon)
605 30th Street
Anacortes, Washington 98221
800-608-4825
www.vitalchoice.com

SPICES, CONDIMENTS, FLAVORED OILS

Penzeys Spice
Retail locations throughout the U.S.
800-741-7787
www.penzeys.com

The Spice House
Retail locations in Illinois and Wisconsin
312-724-0378
www.thespicehouse.com

Tom Douglas
(Spice rubs)
206-448-1193
www.tomdouglas.com

Trader Joe's
(Flavored oils)
Retail locations throughout the U.S.
www.traderjoes.com

Zingerman's
(Spices, oils, vinegars, etc.)
620 Phoenix Drive
Ann Arbor, Michigan 48108
888-636-8162
www.zingermans.com

INDEX

TABLE OF EQUIVALENTS

The exact equivalents in the following table have been rounded for convenience.

LIQUID / DRY MEASUREMENTS	U.S.	METRIC
	1/4 teaspoon	1.25 milliliters
	1/2 teaspoon	2.5 milliliters
	1 teaspoon	5 milliliters
	1 tablespoon (3 teaspoons)	15 milliliters
	1 fluid ounce (2 tablespoons)	30 milliliters
	1/4 cup	60 milliliters
	1/3 cup	80 milliliters
	1/2 cup	120 milliliters
	1 cup	240 milliliters
	1 pint (2 cups)	480 milliliters
	1 quart (4 cups; 32 ounces)	960 milliliters
	1 gallon (4 quarts)	3.84 liters
	1 ounce (by weight)	28 grams
	1 pound	448 grams
	2.2 pounds	1 kilogram

LENGTHS	U.S.	METRIC
	1/8 inch	3 millimeters
	1/4 inch	6 millimeters
	1/2 inch	12 millimeters
	1 inch	2.5 centimeters

OVEN TEMPERATURES	FAHRENHEIT	CELSIUS	GAS
	250	120	1/2
	275	140	1
	300	150	2
	325	160	3
	350	180	4
	375	190	5
	400	200	6
	425	220	7
	450	230	8
	475	240	9
	500	260	10